DATE DUE

The Politics and Practice of Situational Crime Prevention

Ross Homel, editor

CRIME PREVENTION STUDIES, Volume 5

Criminal Justice Press

Monsey, New York, U.S.A.

1996

Published in cooperation with the Centre for Crime Policy and

Public Safety, School of Justice Administration,

Griffith University, Brisbane, Australia

CRIME PREVENTION STUDIES

Ronald V. Clarke, series editor

ISSN (series): 1065-7029

ISBN: 1-881798-06-2

Contents

✦

EDITOR'S INTRODUCTION

by

Ross Homel

Griffith University

This volume of *Crime Prevention Studies* is an "Australian production"—more or less. Most of the authors are Australian, but those who aren't either work in Australia or presented their papers at a Griffith University conference on "Problem Solving For Crime Prevention," held in August 1994. However, despite its origins in the Antipodes, the book is in no sense parochial, limited in scope to Australian problems or case studies. On the contrary, it has been exciting as an editor to help shape a volume that is perhaps more "universal" and certainly more theoretical than its predecessors in this series, raising fundamental questions about the nature and politics of situational crime prevention wherever it is practiced. I would especially like to thank the series editor, Ron Clarke, for the opportunity to prepare this special issue, and for the many ways in which he has assisted in its production.

Given the theme of the Griffith University conference, it is not surprising that there is an emphasis on "problem solving" in the articles by Daniel Gilling, Peter Grabosky, and by Adam Sutton, all of whom made presentations. But it is instructive that these scholars have adopted a rather broad view of what problem solving entails. Indeed, the problem-solving motif grew as I put this volume together, becoming not only more expansive in terms of technical and theoretical issues, but also decisively more political than I had originally envisaged. The political dimension is actually crucial, and its detailed examination by several of the authors in this book is perhaps one of the main advantages of exploring situational prevention from an Australian perspective.

For situational crime prevention is contentious in the Australian context. Despite the impressive achievements of situational approaches in allied fields such as traffic safety and public health, and in crime prevention itself (e.g., Clarke, 1992), most Australian criminologists remain deeply suspicious of an orientation that is viewed as being wedded

Address correspondence to: Ross Homel, School of Justice Administration, Griffith University, Mt. Gravatt Campus, Brisbane, QLD 4111, Australia.

to a conservative crime control agenda emphasizing surveillance of marginalized groups and social exclusion (see, for example, the description of the conservative model of crime prevention in Rob White's chapter). As Adam Sutton comments in his chapter, these suspicions may not simply reflect Australian "sheer bloody-mindedness," but may point to limitations both in situational prevention as it is presently conceived and also in the presuppositions and theoretical orientations of criminologists raised in the tradition of sociological inquiry.

In my experience, advocates of situational approaches tend to be rather hurt by the criticisms of their work, even if they are not particularly surprised. After all, they protest, they are simply trying to make the world a better place for ordinary people—particularly the poor and marginalized, who are the most frequent victims of crime—by really doing something about the problem. They point to the apparently universal failure of "feel good" social improvement programs to make any difference in the crime rate, as well as to the disastrous consequences of a reliance on the criminal justice system through such policies as "three strikes and you're out," to which situational methods offer a genuine alternative (Homel, 1994). They highlight, moreover, the conspicuous successes of environmental, situational and regulatory approaches in fields like traffic safety and public health. Examples of the many successful situational and regulatory measures include seat-belt laws, design rules for vehicles, improved road engineering, randomized traffic law enforcement, needle exchange centers, "safe-sex" techniques emphasizing the use of condoms, better sewerage systems, and the universal provision of clean drinking water. They observe that most of these achievements arose from patient and systematic scientific research combined with broad political support for the ultimate objectives. It is maintained that if the same scientific, problem-solving, non-partisan approach were to be applied to our crime problems, spectacular improvements would be made in the quality of life for citizens who cannot now afford to live in safe suburbs or pay for expensive security systems.

Part of the difficulty with this response is, of course, that it could be said to be based on an oversimplified view of criminological science. As Daniel Gilling observes in his chapter, crime data do not speak for themselves but require interpretation, "... and in the act of interpretation a series of preconceived stereotypical notions about the nature of criminal victimization can come to the fore" (p. 15). These kinds of difficulties are usually not as great when one is analyzing concrete events like traffic injuries, since there is a large degree of consensus about what the problem is and what should be measured. Perhaps more fundamentally, the very notion of "science" that is at the heart of the problem-solving paradigm is contested by sociological critics, who point out that processes like the breaking of a problem in a sequential fashion into "variables," and the attempt to quantify all aspects of a phenomenon, conceal implicit political decisions about how problems should be conceived and analyzed. For example, large-scale probability surveys of crime victimization, in contrast to more qualitative and local studies of victimization, may obscure crucial cultural and social differences in how crime is understood and experienced (Egger et al., 1995).

The problematic nature of the "crime problem" is, according to the critics, a major obstacle in the path of the potential user of "scientific" models of crime prevention. To develop another of Daniel Gilling's arguments, and echoing Gusfield's (1981) study of the culture of public problems, incidents involving private pain, even if they are quite common, only become a public problem if some societal institution is vested with the responsibility for doing something to stop the pain. In the case of crime, the "owners" of the problem are of course the police—who are viewed by the public and by themselves as being responsible for prevention—for reducing the pain of crime victimization. But this means that the police view of reality tends to prevail in problem definitions and in the strategies proposed as solutions, and that other institutions, like schools or big business, can be allowed to "disown" the problem. In theory, perhaps, a researcher can correct for the dominance of the police perspective in problem definition, but in my experience "on the ground," particularly in interagency projects, it is very likely that police will play a major role and be given a lot of the credit for project successes.

What happens "on the ground" in implementation, and how politics and social power enter into all aspects of the prevention process, is a major theme of five of the papers in this volume (Gilling, Grabosky, Sutton, White, and Walters). Peter Grabosky's chapter describes in entertaining detail the many ways in which crime prevention can fail to work, or even increase the crime rate, because the program "engineers" are often "... insufficiently aware of the wider social ecology, the complex, interdependent systems of social life in which the target behavior resides" (p. 13). Grabosky emphasizes such factors as *escalation* (for example, physical barriers may invite defacing), *creative adaptation* (entrepreneurial criminals stay "one step ahead of the law"), and *perverse incentives* ("toys-for-

guns" programs may inadvertently subsidize firearms manufacturers).
Grabosky's main argument is that even successful prevention initiatives
may cause "collateral harm," and that risk analyses should automatically
be included in the planning process. Rigorous policy analysis should be
an essential ingredient of crime prevention, and there is, in his words, "a
role for institutionalized skepticism" (p. 18).

Reading Reece Walters's chapter on multi-agency crime prevention, it
seems that nowhere were skeptics more badly needed than in South
Australia when that state embarked in 1989 on the nation's first coordinated community-based crime prevention program. Adam Sutton, who
was appointed program head for a period, sounded some appropriate
warnings at the beginning when he pointed out that interagency coordination could easily founder on the shoals of competing agency philosophies and struggles over "territory," and that the proposed mixture of
situational and social programs would be difficult to manage and evaluate
(Sutton, 1991). The most striking aspect of Walters's article is his description of the political confusion that surrounded the program, especially
through the operations of the "Coalition Against Crime," a group of 50
politicians, senior public servants and businesspeople who were supposed
to instigate interagency involvement and oversee departmental expenditures. Walters wryly observes that two years after the government had
launched its crime prevention policy, the coalition was still trying to
understand and operationalize the policy using butcher's paper and
professional facilitators! The results at the local level were often chaotic,
with particularly damaging outcomes for Aboriginal communities. According to Walters, interagency programs need not necessarily fail, but must
have specific and measurable goals and be carefully managed to resolve
the inevitable political problems.

The essentially political nature of prevention, and the inherent tension
between social and situational approaches, are also themes of Adam
Sutton's highly readable account of what happens when criminology
students (including police and other criminal justice practitioners) are
required to design and evaluate a crime prevention intervention. Sutton
observes that there is a deep-seated belief among most criminologists and
criminology students that the origins of crime are caused by phenomena
like economic and cultural dislocations, racism, and gender-based power
imbalances, and that any program that does not aim to challenge and
transform such systems is just "tinkering at the edges." His main point,
however, is that groups who, for pragmatic reasons, opt for situational

prevention soon discover the often immense political obstacles involved even in identifying problems, let alone implementing an intervention. As Sutton puts it, "... because crime prevention is about identifying difficulties and trying to bring about change, even the most technical and apparently 'neutral' approaches can prove unsettling to established interests" (p. 13).

The political differences within criminology are thrown into sharp relief by Rob White, who proposes three models of crime prevention: *the conservative model*, which emphasizes crime control, opportunity reduction and rational choice, and tends to focus on protection, surveillance, and conventional street crime; *the liberal model*, which sees crime as a social problem caused by individual or social pathology and focuses on correcting deficits and improving opportunities; and *the radical model*, whose key concept is social justice with a consequent emphasis on the need for political struggle and social change, especially with respect to the crimes of the powerful and the social system that fosters them. White emphasizes that these models are one-sided and exaggerated (political conservatives, for example, may be very concerned about "crime in the suites" as well as "crime in the streets"), but argues that they do reflect broad tendencies at the practical and policy level. His main point is that specific crime prevention strategies are not exclusively the product of any one model, but "how certain measures affect different groups of people depends very much on how they are implemented and the political basis for their particular implementation" (p. 10). Surveillance techniques, for example, could be used by radicals and conservatives alike, but the social content of the practices would be very different.

The authors in this volume who emphasize the inherently political nature of situational prevention present a challenge to advocates of situational approaches that has yet to be answered comprehensively. In some recent work, Ron Clarke and I (Clarke and Homel, 1996) did not undertake this task directly, but perhaps did something that is a necessary first step: we attempted to move situational prevention from an almost exclusive preoccupation with the physical environment to consider aspects of the psychological and social environments. Central to our analysis was the attempt to identify and classify techniques of prevention that blunt the effects of the kinds of "moral neutralization techniques" described many years ago by Sykes and Matza (1957) in their study of delinquency, and more recently by Bandura (1977) in his social learning analysis of aggression. We also relabeled the three columns of the original classification to emphasize the perceptual basis of the situational approach, and to bring it more explicitly into line with the rational choice perspective.

Our rather cautious attempt to overcome some of the limitations, as we saw them, in conventional situational prevention thinking met with two main responses from our colleagues, even before the paper was published: they either loathed it or they loved it. Richard Wortley's chapter is a creative attempt to move beyond such polarized positions, by separating more clearly measures designed to manipulate internal controls (guilt) from those designed to manipulate social controls (shame). Wortley proposes a reorganization of the "guilt-inducing" approach to include such measures as *increasing victim worth*—e.g., victim cooperation strategies— (see Indermaur's chapter in this volume), and the addition of a range of measures to increase social controls, such as *reducing social approval* (e.g., the non-televising of "streaking") and *reducing imitation* (e.g., discrediting models that encourage crime).

Wortley's paper brings situational prevention even more closely into line with the deterrence literature (e.g., Grasmick and Bursik, 1990) and also with the rational choice perspective (Cornish and Clarke, 1986), and is clearly a significant theoretical advance, even if one is left with the feeling that every one of his eight new techniques deserves a paper of its own. Whether or not one agrees with every detail of Wortley's chapter (or of Clarke and Homel's), a major advantage of incorporating aspects of the non-physical environment into situational analysis is that one has at one's disposal a wider repertoire of techniques that can help to resolve some of the political impasses faced by prevention workers who, under present circumstances, often have to choose between distasteful "fortress society" techniques and social prevention programs of doubtful effectiveness.

Two empirical studies conclude this volume. Each study is of the decision-making processes of violent offenders (robbers or burglars), and each illustrates the value for prevention research of analyzing crime events from the offender's (and the victim's) perspective. The studies therefore illustrate the approach advocated by Clarke and Homel (1996), who propose an emphasis on *perceived* effort, *perceived* risk, and *anticipated* rewards.

Based on his analysis of 88 offenders and 10 victims involved in robbery and property crime in Western Australia, David Indermaur concludes that offenders are principally concerned with "getting the goods and getting away," and that in general the best way of preventing violence during the course of a crime is to make it more attractive to the offender to avoid confrontation or to flee the scene as quickly as possible. In particular, often the most effective strategy is for the victim not to offer resistance and even to facilitate the offender's escape. The basis of this controversial advice is the finding that offenders often feel angry with the victim for not conforming to the "victim role." Non-resistance or cooperation may be one way of "increasing the victim's worth," in Wortley's terms. Indermaur's fascinating analysis illustrates the value for prevention research of integrating offender and victim perspectives, where it can be done. It also has important implications for social policy, suggesting that moves in some places to encourage homeowners and business proprietors to protect themselves with firearms may not deter offenders, but instead increase the number of violent encounters.

Shona Morrison's chapter on the decision-making practices of commercial armed robbers is based on a study of 88 offenders incarcerated in the U.K. This is the same number interviewed by David Indermaur in Western Australia, but the interview data are supplemented by police records of over 1,000 cases occurring in London in 1990. The paper is notable for its methodological rigor, and particularly for the thoughtful section on the validity of offenders' accounts of their decision making. A notable finding of the study is the degree of *rationality* that is evident when offenders' own interpretations of their actions are thoroughly investigated. Among the many important details are that serious repeat offenders are often satisfied with stealing small sums, and that the offenders in general had quite realistic ideas concerning what they were likely to gain from a robbery and what the risks of apprehension were.

Although it is important to remember that no information from the study was available about *potential* offenders who are deterred by existing prevention measures, Morrison's analysis suggests that there are no simple ways of reducing offenses committed by offenders who have embarked on robbery as a central element of an active criminal career. She suggests that further target-hardening and other situational measures may be the best avenue to pursue. But she also hints, intriguingly, that in the long term more may be gained by exploring questions such as how people develop a readiness to offend, and how they get their information about robbery as a crime. Morrison implies that effective prevention may involve social or developmental programs (Farrington, 1995), as well as situational measures. But perhaps a broader view of situational prevention, along the lines proposed by Ron Clarke and myself and by Richard

Wortley, would also suggest practical and more immediate ways of manipulating the psychological or social environments of these offenders.

This volume will have achieved the objectives set for it if it stimulates more creative thinking about situational prevention, and sensitizes both advocates and critics to its inherently political nature. In particular, it is my hope that in place of the present standoff between adherents of situational and social approaches we may see creative dialogue and the development of better theories to underpin the practice of prevention.

REFERENCES

Bandura, A. (1977). *Social Learning Theory.* Englewood Cliffs, NJ: Prentice-Hall.

Clarke, R.V. (ed.) (1992). *Situational Crime Prevention: Successful Case Studies.* Albany, NY: Harrow and Heston.

Clarke, R.V. and R. Homel (in press, 1996). "A Revised Classification of Situational Crime Prevention Techniques." In: S.P. Lab (ed.), *Crime Prevention at the Crossroads.* Cincinnati, OH: Anderson.

Cornish, D. and R.V. Clarke (eds.) (1986). *The Reasoning Criminal: Rational Choice Perspectives on Offending.* New York, NY: Springer-Verlag.

Egger, S.; D. Brown and G. Travis (1995). "Counting Crime: Are Victim Surveys the Answer?" In: D. Brereton (ed.), *Crime Victim Surveys in Australia: Conference Proceedings.* Brisbane, AUS: Criminal Justice Commission.

Farrington, D. (1995). "Key Issues in the Integration of Motivational and Opportunity-Reducing Crime Prevention Strategies." In P.H. Wikström, R.V. Clarke and J. McCord (eds.), *Integrating Crime Prevention Strategies: Propensity and Opportunity.* Stockholm, Sweden: National Council for Crime Prevention.

Grasmick, H.G. and R.J. Bursik (1990). "Conscience, Significant Others and Rational Choice." *Law and Society Review* 34:837-861.

Gusfield, J.R. (1981). *The Culture of Public Problems: Drinking-Driving and the Symbolic Order.* Chicago, IL: University of Chicago Press.

Homel, R. (1994). "Flawed Order: The Administration of Justice in a 'Get Tough' Era." *Inaugural Professorial Lecture delivered at Griffith University,* Brisbane, AUS, June 2, 1994.

Sutton, A. (1991). "The Bonnemaison Model: Theory and Application." In: B. Halstead (ed.) *Youth Crime Prevention—Proceedings of a Policy Forum held 28 and 29 August 1990.* Canberra: Australian Institute of Criminology.

Sykes, G. and D. Matza (1957). "Techniques of Neutralization: A Theory of Delinquency." *American Journal of Sociology* 22:664-670.

PROBLEMS WITH THE
PROBLEM-ORIENTED APPROACH

by
Daniel Gilling
University of Plymouth

Abstract: This paper subjects the problem-oriented approach to crime prevention to critical scrutiny. Though acknowledged as a theoretically coherent and
potentially highly promising technique of crime control, questions are raised
about the extent to which the ambitions of the approach are likely to be
realised in the process of translation from the realm of ideas to the realm of
action. In particular, three broad kinds of barriers are considered that may
stand in the way of realisation of the approach's full potential: the problems
of responsibility, of politics, and of identification. The paper draws upon
empirical material from Britain but raises issues of international relevance.

INTRODUCTION

This paper considers the background to the emergence of the problem-
oriented approach, together with its basic assumptions. It then goes on to
look at a range of factors that stand in the way of the realisation of this
highly rationalistic model of crime control. Particular attention is given to
how these factors affect notions of what is or is not to be regarded as a
problem suitable to this approach. These factors must be constantly borne
in mind and planned for by those developing this highly promising
approach to crime control. It should be noted that problem-oriented crime
prevention is not synonymous with problem-oriented policing (Goldstein,
1990), since the focus of the latter is wider than just crime.

Address for correspondence: Daniel Gilling, Department of Applied Social Science,
University of Plymouth, Drake Circus, Plymouth PL4 8AA, U.K.

THE BACKGROUND

The sense of utilitarian optimism surrounding the capacity of the public sector to make good its promises of eliminating key social problems such as crime was shattered in the 1970s by the emergence of stinging critiques from both right- and left-wing constituencies, and an economic crisis that rendered the logic of such critiques irresistible. However, over the last two decades there have emerged two distinct phenomena that have augured well for both the emergence and future development of crime prevention. The first of these has been a preparedness to question the efficacy of many of public policy's "sacred cows," including, within the criminal justice domain, the "3 P's" of police, prisons and probation. In the long-distance race of crime control, this has enabled crime prevention to move up from the position of back-marker to one of the leading pack.

Following in the political and economic wake of the first, the second notable phenomenon of the past 20 years has been the emergence of the "new managerialist" paradigm. Definitions of this paradigm are varied and disputed, but the key point is that it has brought a new currency to public policies, which must now be justified increasingly according to the imperatives of economy, efficiency and effectiveness, or the general rubric of "value for money." Accompanying this development, and as part of a trend wherein public organisations have taken their cue from the most successful private ones (Peters and Waterman, 1982), the service user or consumer has emerged as a much more important player in the policy process, forcing organisations to pay considerably more attention to the questions of service and product quality.

Crime prevention has reflected this movement in many ways, most notably by enhancing the position of the victim relative to the offender or society as a consumer of criminal justice services. In particular, crime prevention strengthens the victim or potential victim's hand by replacing generic, undiscriminating and unfocused crime control practices with ones that are tailored and targeted toward the specific needs of specific groups. In the light of findings from numerous national and local victimisation studies, which demonstrate that the risk of victimisation is concentrated in specific geographical areas, social groups or even individuals, the prospects of crime prevention offering enhanced value for money and quality are generally good.

Targeting is the key mechanism here. Not only does it represent an enhanced consumer-responsiveness that is likely to bring positive evaluations of quality, it also acts as a means of rationing whereby scarce crime prevention resources can be focused where they are most needed, in the same way that means-testing acts as a selective rationing mechanism for social security benefits. Targeting, then, is simultaneously about economy, efficiency, and effectiveness, and as the economic imperative continues to dictate the pattern of public spending in the mid-1990s, it is essential that we spend our crime prevention budgets wisely and well.

THE PROBLEM-ORIENTED APPROACH

Although there is still a place for generalised publicity campaigns and the provision of specialist advice and information from police crime prevention officers, the now-familiar problem-oriented approach to crime prevention has begun to move to the fore as our major strategy, typified by the situational model of crime prevention pioneered by the British Home Office in the mid-1970s (Mayhew et al., 1976). The core of this approach is its dynamism and flexibility: it is problem- rather than practice-oriented, which means there are no preconceived notions of how best to tackle the specific crime problem under investigation. Instead, the object is to fully research all of the information available about the situation of a particular crime problem, drawing data from as many different agency sources as is both possible and necessary. From this research, a full picture of the crime problem should be possible, enabling those involved in the exercise to pinpoint exactly where, and often also when, a preventive strategy needs to be directed. Thereafter, it is a case of deciding what this strategy should actually be, and then implementing it together with a built-in monitoring system that can subsequently be used for purposes of fine-tuning and program evaluation. The process is quintessentially rational, with each step following on logically from the preceding one.

In theory, the model appears ideal, facilitating the development of a range of innovative prevention strategies that are as varied as the crime problems they seek to tackle. Indeed, many who have followed its logic have scored spectacular successes in the fight against crime. However, as with all theories of rational action, the problem-oriented model has its limitations. As Max Weber (1978) so ably demonstrated, there are more forms of action than the purely rational, and there is more than one form of rationality. To borrow from Weberian terminology, the problem-oriented approach is essentially an ideal type.

Consequently, the model is not always faithfully or unproblematically pursued. Starting at its end, for example, it has been noted that a lack of attention has sometimes been paid to both monitoring and evaluation—as if the implementation were the end rather than the means to the end (U.K. Home Office, 1986). Where this does occur, the impact of crime prevention strategies is often insufficiently understood, and this can prove to be both frustrating and problematic for those seeking successful replications elsewhere (Tilley, 1993). Indeed, even where initiatives are evaluated, such evaluations can be misread. As a good example of this, Pease (1994) offers cases where research into initiatives involving Neighbourhood Watch have been read as "theory failure" when a more diligent reading of the research would show clearly that, in fact, "implementation failure" was to blame. Elsewhere, a number of other studies have demonstrated the various practical, political and organisational influences that render policy formulation, and particularly implementation, a good deal less of an exact science than the rational model might sometimes suppose (Hope, 1985; Sampson et al., 1988).

This paper follows in the tradition of those that have sought to uncover some of the difficulties that can stand in the way of the realisation of the rationalistic problem-oriented approach to crime prevention. However, whilst most attention has hitherto been addressed to the end of the process, and particularly to implementation, the remainder of this paper switches attention to the very beginning of that process. That is, the concept of problem-orientation is itself taken to be problematic. For conceptual clarity, this paper is divided into three sections, each of which overlap a good deal.

THE PROBLEM OF RESPONSIBILITY

The literature on problem-oriented crime prevention—or whatever it is specifically labelled as—begins at the same methodological point. Thus, Clarke (1992) describes stage one as "the collection of data about the nature and dimensions of the specific crime problem" (p.5); Ekblom (1988) identifies it as "obtaining data on crime problems" (p.6); and Berry and Carter (1992) begin with the assertion that "there should be a clear understanding of the problem being addressed" (p.27).

Behind each of these prescriptions lies the assumption that some crime phenomenon has indeed attained the status of a problem. It is an assumption that lies at the heart of academic research discourse, insofar as the crime being investigated is "the research problem." But one should not necessarily conclude from this that others share this sense of "problem," for it more usually may be taken to mean something that has become intolerable, and about which something more should be done.

In the crime control field, if we look at what is currently being done our attention tends to fall first upon the police. For a crime to be regarded as a particular problem in the latter sense, either the police or the public must elevate it to that status. Herein, however, lies the first difficulty, for in much the same way that neo-conservative governments continue to bemoan the alleged "dependency culture" bred by the institutions of the welfare state, so one could similarly bemoan a dependency culture in crime control, wherein both responsibility and expertise are deferred to the police.

This has happened in part because the police have succeeded in convincing the public of their professional status, in much the same way that doctors have. There is much difference between the two occupational groups. However, at least until comparatively recently, both have been able to circumscribe their own work as a consequence of having persuaded us of their expertise in tackling crime and ill health, respectively. There is nothing wrong with this so long as professions do indeed deliver what they promise, but it has become increasingly evident that this is not the case in the 1990s.

The professions are now under attack, but their defences are strong. In the context of crime control, for something to be regarded as a problem that might then usher in the problem-oriented approach, the police would have to recognise that existing strategies are not holding the line against crime. However, given the sensitive nature of law and order in British politics, for example, and the fear that each of the main parties has of the other holding the higher ground, the police have been largely successful in claiming that existing strategies can hold the line, given sufficient resources to do so. Consequently, until very recently the police have been successful in claiming extra resources to get "more bobbies on the beat," despite overwhelming evidence (Clarke and Hough, 1980) that this has a very marginal impact on crime.

The police, then, have been quite successful in defining crime control in their own terms. And since in Britain they are the only agency to carry a statutory responsibility for crime prevention—one that played a major part in their bid for legitimation in 1829, and arguably continues to do so—they have been able to use the concept's definitional elasticity to encompass their own preferred ways of working. With a heavy emphasis on "reactive" methods, these ways bear only a slight relation to the original meaning of the term in what Reiner (1992) calls "the scarecrow function" of visible uniformed patrolling (calling for more bobbies on the beat does not necessarily mean that this is where they will be deployed), or to what we would regard as "true" crime prevention today.

The police are no different than any other modern large bureaucratic organisation insofar as they display Weberian tendencies of conservatism and resistance to change. Consequently, despite the many changes of form that have occurred over the past couple of decades, the content remains pretty much the same repertoire of traditional responses. Again, like most organisations, there is a tendency to satisfice rather than maximise—a tendency that the new managerialism has not yet successfully tackled. Hence, for example, the difficulties that officers have encountered when urged to make the cultural shift to problem-oriented policing (Goldstein, 1990). Often the requisite perceived need to change is not there.

One might argue that the development of specialist police crime prevention departments contradicts this point by providing a more focused concern with crime prevention and a greater willingness to change. However, the prospects of their inculcating a greater sense of responsibility within the police for use of the problem-oriented approach to crime prevention remains limited. As research by Harvey et al. (1989) has demonstrated, this is because crime prevention departments are largely "ghettoised" within the police. As Johnston et al. (1993) add, on the basis of their research in one London Metropolitan Police Division, "the delivery of this specialist crime prevention service was not coordinated with the rest of the policing service, nor was it necessarily planned to focus on the Division's main priorities for crime reduction" (p.5).

Furthermore, in some forces crime prevention officers are insufficiently equipped for their specialist tasks as a consequence of being untrained. Even where they are, a major difficulty remains in that forces with the highest crime levels have the fewest officers, whilst the general use of such officers tends to be focused upon those (typically middle-class) areas where they are least needed.

Therefore, when the public seeks to rely upon the police, the result is unlikely to be particularly conducive to the development of the problem-oriented approach to crime prevention. Of course, not all of the public do so rely: the growth in the domestic security technology market, in vigilantism, and in the participation of volunteers in the criminal justice system (Mawby and Gill, 1990) all bear testimony to a growing public acknowledgement that crime is a problem about which something else needs to be done. However, whilst these are potentially significant resources to aid crime preventive effort, they are not normally harnessed into a concerted problem-oriented approach. For reasons that will be considered in more detail below, Pease (1994) suggests that just such a harnessing might profitably take place between victim support services and crime prevention.

The public, then, does not always take the responsibility for crime control that it could, and even when it does it is rarely well-directed (the best protected households are probably those least at risk). Private business interests, however, are no less culpable, frequently displaying a marked reluctance to invest in crime prevention. As Pease (1994) argues "[t]here is no doubt a threshold of cost above which simple crime prevention will come into play in commercial judgements, but that threshold is massively above the point at which the crime represents a significant social problem" (p.60).

Once again, different notions of problem prevail: petty crimes such as shoplifting (Ekblom, 1986) can affect profit margins only marginally, but they can affect society more markedly by incurring significant public expense once the wheels of justice are brought into motion. Nowhere is this disregard of the broader costs of crime better demonstrated than in the credit card (Levi et al., 1991) or the automobile industries, where, as both Clarke (1992) and Pease (1994) observe, there is little incentive at present to design out crime, despite the simplicity of the preventive measures. Whether changes to vehicle excise duty or insurance premiums can improve this situation remains untested, and it would be interesting to see whether the Home Office's recent decision to publish a detailed breakdown of thefts by vehicle type will spur vehicle manufacturers into action. As Clarke (1992) points out, the long term focus on crime control really necessitates a permanent in-house capability, and until this can be achieved the business sector is unlikely to become a prominent player in the problem-oriented approach to crime prevention.

In Britain, the establishment of the formally independent body Crime Concern in 1988 was in fact intended to help spread the crime prevention message into the private sector, although it has since broadened its remit and there is as yet no research to suggest whether or not it has been effective to this end. One possible source of difficulty is that the body's independent status and need for finance drives it into the private sector in search of sponsorship more than practical commitment, thereby risking goal displacement from crime prevention to public relations. This area requires further research.

THE PROBLEM OF POLITICS

The problem of politics is closely entwined with that of responsibility insofar as it points to a range of attitudes and dispositions that are hindrances in the search for a problem-oriented approach to crime prevention.

Perhaps the most fundamental underlying assumption of the approach is that it requires a change, either by getting those who never thought of crime as their concern to take on a new responsibility, or urging those used to tackling crime in one way to think of an alternative, more effective way. Change is, however, never straightforward, not least because of the vested interests that support the status quo so long as it brings them tangible benefits.

There is little doubt that the problem-oriented approach to crime prevention has made significant headway since the paradigm-breaking publication of *Crime as Opportunity* in 1976 (Mayhew et al.), but even so there are some serious barriers to its development. It is, for example, unfortunate that the rise of this form of crime prevention has coincided with the rise of neo-conservativism. A central element of the latter movement has been the creation of a populist platform out of the law-and-order theme, which is considerably less interested in crime prevention than in the "get-tough" rhetoric of retributivism and in strengthening the hand of the police, despite the fact that both were implicated in the "nothing works" crisis of the 1970s. Consequently, support for crime prevention is not as strong as it could be, when vote-winning comes before problem-solving.

Since the mid-1980s the right has lost some of its grip on the law-and-order question, to the extent that the criminal justice credentials of the British Labour Party are now, if anything, more convincing, and thus more likely to attract populist support around the slogan "get tough on crime; get tough on the causes of crime." However, this has the potential to be equally detrimental to the future of the problem-oriented approach, as one

ideological lens is merely substituted for another. This time the preconceived diagnosis of fecklessness and indiscipline is replaced or augmented
by one of deterministic liberal social reformism.

In many ways one can see this process already under way within the
Home Office, which has become much more accommodating of what I have
argued elsewhere (Gilling, 1994) to be the less exact science of social crime
prevention within the nominally problem-oriented frameworks of such
initiatives as the Safer Cities Programme. This shift may be attributed
partly to Clarke's (1992) observation that some problem-oriented strategies have faced a cool reception, whereby incrementalist reformism has
been misrepresented as, at worst, an Orwellian nightmare, and, at best,
a would-be hero with the tragic flaw of displacement. It is also in part the
consequence of the opening up of crime prevention, via a partnership
approach, to social policy-type agencies that lack a clear problem-oriented
sense of direction in this area.

Further difficulties exist at what may be termed the mezzo-level, where,
as the above point implies, agencies that should have an interest in crime
prevention are brought into the infrastructure of a problem-oriented
approach but fail to make the necessary accommodation in their traditional roles. Traditional rather than rational action, for example, requires
the probation service to be hostile to crime prevention strategies that
appear to lack a "caring" face, or the police to be resistant to strategies
that disempower them by making them superfluous. In contrast to the
rational orientation of problem orientation, these traditional perspectives
share different assumptive worlds and speak different languages.

A genuine problem-oriented approach requires the sorts of collaborative relationships that do not square with the reality of organisational
behaviour. His work may now be a bit dated, but Benson's (1975) conception of the inter-organisational network as a political economy ably fits
the usual pattern of organisational defensiveness and mutual suspicion,
especially within a general climate of resource scarcity. Pressure to
develop a problem orientation often carries with it an implication that
things have not been done well in the past—something to which organisations or occupational groups are understandably loath to admit.

There is also the issue of goal displacement, whereby the objective of
getting agencies together to consider a problem-oriented approach is
effectively relegated to a secondary consideration as agencies seek instead
to take full advantage of the public relations value of being seen to be

contributing to a collaborative effort against crime. It most certainly happens, as once again populist political agendas get in the way.

Finally, it is worth drawing attention to the politics of the victim. A problem orientation is more feasible in regard to crimes with certain categories of victim, who are more likely to come to our attention than others. As Pease (1994) suggests, for example, victims of violence often lack the political influence of powerful propertied interests, whose economic muscle and lobbying potential are far more likely to succeed in drawing attention to their plight. In a similar vein, victimless crimes by their very nature have no victim lobby, and are consequently less likely to become the focus of a problem-oriented approach. However, in such cases the resource savings afforded to law enforcement agencies (as victims by proxy) might provide an alternative motivation for action. Drug misuse provides an obvious example.

THE PROBLEM OF IDENTIFICATION

The final area to be considered is perhaps also the most significant of the barriers that stand in the way of the realisation of a problem orientation. There is an assumption in the rational model that once participants are focused upon a particular crime issue, they should be able to rationally scrutinise and analyse the available data and come up with an accurate diagnosis of both problem and solution, although there is always scope for fine-tuning. However, as with the hope that people will take responsibility for crime prevention and that ulterior motives will not cloud their judgement, this is based upon a lack of appreciation of what can actually happen.

A good example of this, which has an obvious overlap with the problem of politics, is provided by Stanko (1990). In a short critique of crime prevention, Stanko questions the wisdom of some of the publicity-oriented elements of British crime prevention policy. Although recent improvements have been made in crime prevention advice and publicity in this area, Stanko points out that much of this advice is premised upon a misdiagnosis of the problem. That is to say, with regard to the issues of personal and sexual violence, much of the advice is based upon a stereotypical notion of an "external enemy"—the unknown stranger who is the object of so many of our fears. In fact, as a closer analysis of these crimes demonstrates, the majority of such offenders are "the enemies within"—people who are known to their victims and who may often live with them. The sad irony is that protecting oneself from the external enemy can end up increasing one's vulnerability to the enemy within.

Stanko (1990) attributes such an oversight to a patriarchy-induced myopia regarding the true causes of violence against women, the elimination of which would lead to a clearer understanding of this kind of problem and the nature of potentially preventive solutions. This alerts us to the possibility of myopia existing elsewhere within general strategies of crime prevention, and two further examples spring to mind. The first relates to thefts from retail premises, which are often assumed to emanate from the depredations of customers, when in fact the heaviest damage is often wrought by the employees of such premises. Preventive solutions directed in the wrong place because of commonsense assumptions are potentially highly wasteful.

A second example may be found in the numerous estate-based crime prevention projects that are oriented to the improvement of security and surveillance against outsiders. There is a failure to acknowledge that the potential offenders may live amongst the victims, and may indeed be one and the same person on occasion. Crime analyses have to make allowances for such possibilities, as was the case with the Kirkholt Project (Forrester et al., 1988), where the preventive measures that were introduced allowed for the possibility that some of the large number of cash meter thefts could indeed be "own goals," as police slang so prosaically puts it.

In all these examples, misdiagnoses of crime problems can result from the failure to research the characteristics of crimes in sufficient depth, although this is not always possible anyway given the limitations of data collection in the crime field. More importantly, the examples demonstrate that the data does not speak for itself—it requires interpretation, and in the act of interpretation a series of preconceived stereotypical notions about the nature of criminal victimisation can come to the fore. This leads us to a closer consideration of how we gather our information about crime.

The principal sources of data are police statistics which, as is by now well-known, depend heavily upon what victims and others choose to report to the police, and what the police then subsequently choose to record. They are artifacts of a social process rather than an objective representation of a range of actions that are classified as crimes in a given place at a given time. What the statistics indicate as a problem, and what really is a problem, may be two different things.

Underreported crimes, such as some crimes of violence and many minor uninsured property offences, represent a case in point here. These crimes may often be excluded from consideration as preventable problems because there is no available data on them. Victimisation studies can give us some idea as to their prevalence, but they cannot provide us with the sort of precise information upon which the problem-oriented approach is predicated. Moreover, since these crimes are underreported, it would be exceedingly difficult to discern the effects of any preventive activities upon them. And given the primacy of the need to demonstrate effectiveness, one can understand the reluctance to focus upon underreported crimes. The retort that such crimes cannot be regarded as real problems if they are not reported is unacceptably glib.

It is, however, important to recognise that the vagaries of reporting behaviour can significantly impair the functioning of the problem-oriented approach, which is evidently suited to crimes with the highest reporting rates. Indeed, when Heal and Laycock (1986) suggest that situational crime prevention is not appropriate for violent crimes, which do not appear so clustered in time and space as property offences, this is in effect the very point they are making. However, as Clarke (1992) rightly points out, this does not actually mean that situational techniques cannot be effective for such crimes.

Moving on, there remain many more difficulties associated with the identification of crime problems. The data that the police possess essentially facilitates the identification of crime "hot spots," represented most crudely by pins in a map. In some areas there will be relatively few pins, whilst in others there will be many—it is unclear at precisely what point, or at how many pins, an area is ascribed a problem status. The implication is that there is a threshold beyond which crime can no longer be regarded as tolerable, although such a threshold is presumably arbitrary. This can be awkward, and is not necessarily the most effective way of determining priorities. A parallel can be drawn with urban policies that seek to divert resources to the most deprived areas but in so doing deny resources to equally deprived people living outside such areas.

The work of Farrell and Pease (1993) on repeat victimisation elaborates upon this point. They argue that crime prevention resources are rarely focused upon those most in need—repeat victims—but that such a focus would prove to be the most effective and socially acceptable means of rationing scarce resources. This is because of a clear statistical pattern across a number of different crimes that show a disproportionately high number of offenses as repeat victimisations, most of which are likely to reoccur within a relatively short time of the initial victimisation. Consequently, victimisation is the best predictor of future risk of victimisation, and this is therefore where crime preventive effort should be concentrated.

At present this is not usually the case because of a basic misapprehension in the use of the problem-oriented approach. As Farrell and Pease (1993) point out, crime prevention is difficult in comparison to other areas of public policy by virtue of the fact that its object of concern is not present states but future risk. Police statistics, however, measure past and present states, and in so doing often convey the erroneous assumption that it is areas at risk, and not individuals. As a result, much crime preventive effort is wasted, again as a result of a sort of myopia stemming from a lack of appreciation of the full complexity of crime patterns.

SUMMARY

The object of this paper has been to draw attention to a range of difficulties that can lie in the way of the realisation of the rationalistic problem-oriented approach to crime prevention. It is not intended as a criticism of the problem-oriented approach *per se*. On the contrary, it is evident that the potential of the approach is enormous, and that there have already been many examples of successful practice. Followed correctly, this approach provides the best opportunity of making a significant and lasting impact upon the growing levels of crime that have been a characteristic feature of most of the post-war developed world, and thus it offers liberation from the "nothing works" pessimism that still lies beneath the surface of crime control discourse. However, given its tenuous position as a relatively new paradigm, the problem-oriented approach cannot afford to underestimate the strength of the opposition manifested in traditional perspectives, alternative agendas, and the limitations of existing data sources and interpretative frameworks. There is a considerable amount of pressure being exerted on the problem-oriented approach to be stretched in a particular political direction (O'Malley, 1994; Sutton, 1994). Whether the approach can retain its rational integrity in the face of this pressure remains its most vital challenge for the 1990s.

REFERENCES

Benson, J. (1975). "The Inter-organisational Network as a Political Economy." *Administrative Science Quarterly* 20(2):229-249.

Berry G. and M. Carter (1992). *Assessing Crime Prevention Initiatives: The First Steps.* London; UK: Home Office Crime Prevention Unit.

Clarke, R. (1992). *Situational Crime Prevention: Successful Case Studies.* Albany, NY: Harrow & Heston.

—— and M. Hough. (eds.) (1980). *The Effectiveness of Policing.* Farnborough, UK: Gower.

Ekblom, P. (1986). *The Prevention of Shop Theft.* London, UK: Home Office Crime Prevention Unit.

—— (1988). *Getting the Best out of Crime Analysis.* London, UK: Home Office Crime Prevention Unit.

Farrell, G. and K. Pease (1993). *Once Bitten, Twice Bitten: Repeat Victimisation and its Implications for Crime Prevention.* London, UK: Home Office Crime Prevention Unit.

Forrester, D., K. Pease and M. Chatterton (1988). *The Kirkholt Burglary Prevention Demonstration Project; Phase One.* London, UK: Home Office Crime Prevention Unit.

Gilling, D. (1994). "Multi-Agency Crime Prevention In Britain: The Problem of Combining Situational and Social Strategies." In: R. Clarke (ed.), *Crime Prevention Studies, Vol. 3.* Monsey, NY: Criminal Justice Press.

Goldstein, H. (1990). *Problem-Oriented Policing.* New York, NY: McGraw Hill.

Harvey, L., P. Grimshaw and K. Pease (1989). "Crime Prevention Delivery: the Work of CPOs." In: R. Morgan and D. Smith (eds.), *Coming to Terms With Policing.* London, UK: Routledge.

Heal, K. and G. Laycock (eds.) (1986). *Situational Crime Prevention: From Theory Into Practice.* London, UK: Her Majesty's Stationery Office.

Hope, T. (1985). *Implementing Crime Prevention Measures.* London, UK: Her Majesty's Stationery Office.

Johnson, V., J. Shapland and P. Wiles (1993). *Developing Police Crime Prevention: Management and Organisational Change.* London, UK: Home Office Crime Prevention Unit.

Levi, M., P. Bissell and T. Richardson (1991). *The Prevention of Cheque and Credit Card Fraud.* London, UK: Home Office Crime Prevention Unit.

Mawby, R. and M. Gill (1990). *Volunteers in the Criminal Justice System.* Milton Keynes, UK: Open University Press.

Mayhew, P., R. Clarke, A. Sturman and J. Hough (1976). *Crime As Opportunity.* London, UK: Home Office.

O'Malley, P. (1994). "Neo-Liberal Crime Control—Political Agendas and the Future of Crime Prevention in Australia." In: D. Chappell and P. Wilson (eds.), *The Australian Criminal Justice System*. Sydney, AUS: Butterworths.

Pease, K. (1994). "Crime Prevention." In: M. Maguire, R. Morgan and R. Reiner (eds.), *The Oxford Handbook of Criminology*. Oxford, UK: Oxford University Press.

Peters, T. and S. Waterman (1982). *In Search of Excellence*. New York, NY: Harper & Row.

Reiner, R. (1992). *The Politics of the Police*. Brighton, UK: Harvester Wheatsheaf.

Sampson, A., P. Stubbs, D. Smith, G. Pearson and H. Blagg (1988). "Crime, Localities and the Multi-Agency Approach." *British Journal of Criminology* 28(4):478-493.

Stanko, E. (1990). "When Precaution is Normal: A Feminist Critique of Crime Prevention." In: L. Gelsthorpe and A. Morris (eds.), *Feminist Perspectives in Criminology*. Milton Keynes, UK: Open University Press.

Sutton, A. (1994). "Crime Prevention: Promise or Threat." *Australian and New Zealand Journal of Criminology* 27:21-24.

Tilley, N. (1993). *After Kirkholt: Theory, Method and Results in Replication Evaluations*. London, UK: Home Office Crime Prevention Unit.

U.K. Home Office (1986). *Crime Prevention Initiatives in England and Wales*. London, UK: Crime Prevention Unit.

Weber, M. (1978). *Economy and Society*. Berkeley, CA: University of California Press.

UNINTENDED CONSEQUENCES OF CRIME PREVENTION

by

P. N. Grabosky

The Australian National University

and

The Australian Institute of Criminology

Abstract: A review identifies unintended consequences of crime prevention initiatives that may nullify their effectiveness or produce counterproductive results. A typology of regressive outcomes includes crime escalation, displacement, overdeterrence, and perverse incentives. Causes of these negative externalities include failures in analysis, planning and implementation. However, safeguards are possible to avoid many of the unintended consequences.

PART ONE: INTRODUCTION

It borders on the fatuous to suggest that programs designed to prevent crime do not always succeed. Regardless of success or failure, some programs generate what economists would refer to as social costs, or "negative externalities." The ways in which crime prevention programs may become derailed are numerous and diverse, as are the generic pathologies that give rise to these derailments. The present essay pursues this theme by attempting an overview of the ways in which crime prevention initiatives may defeat themselves or otherwise inflict collateral damage. The focus goes beyond those initiatives that simply fail to have their intended effect. Rather, we are concerned with initiatives that either

Address correspondence to: P.N. Grabosky, P.O. Box 54, Deakin, 2600, A.C.T., Australia.

backfire entirely, in effect making things worse, or those resulting in significant harm that offsets many or most of the benefits that the original initiatives may produce. Our concern rests primarily with institutions operating "upstream" of prosecution, delivering what is generally referred to as "situational" or "social" crime prevention, although downstream examples may be invoked where illustrative.

Despite its apparent preoccupation with failure, this essay has been written in a constructive spirit. Just as the study of engineering failures does not imply that society should forsake the use of bridges or buildings, the study of crime prevention failures does not suggest that crime prevention efforts should be abandoned. The analysis of engineering failures enables the subsequent construction of stronger bridges and taller buildings; the analysis of crime prevention failure can lead to the design and implementation of better crime prevention programs. Thus the objective of this essay is not to cast a pall of pessimism over the enterprise of crime prevention, but rather to foster more analytical rigor in the planning, implementation, and evaluation of crime prevention activity.

The paper has three main parts. Part II presents a typology of regressive outcomes that may flow from crime prevention policies, to include such phenomena as escalation, overdeterrence, and the generation of perverse incentives. Part III seeks to explain the etiology of these negative externalities in terms of such phenomena as planning and implementation failures. Part IV suggests principles and safeguards that, if heeded by those in a position to formulate and implement crime prevention policy, will serve to reduce the risk of undesirable unintended consequences.

PART TWO: VARIETIES OF COUNTERPRODUCTIVE CRIME PREVENTION

Escalation

Ironies abound in criminal justice. G. Marx (1981) reminds us that authorities may, in the course of various strategies to combat crime, actually *produce* crime. He identifies three basic situations in which policing strategies may contribute to crime. The first of these—and the only one to concern us here—is *escalation*. In some cases, apparently well-designed programs with the best of intentions may do more harm than good. One of the earliest and most celebrated delinquency prevention initiatives was undertaken more than 50 years ago in the Boston area. The Cambridge-Somerville Youth Study, as it was known, provided services to at-risk youths, including academic tutoring, recreational opportunities, family support, health services, and counselling. The program made eminent theoretical sense, and was praised by participants and administrators alike. Unfortunately, a follow-up study of program participants and a control group (McCord, 1978) revealed that the program failed on a number of criteria. Not only were participants more likely than members of the control group to offend, but they compared unfavourably on a number of additional criteria including mortality, stress-related disease, and evidence of mental illness and alcoholism.

Other forms of escalation are less subtle and more immediately apparent. The construction of physical barriers may invite their defacing or destruction. The frustration that results from blocked criminal opportunity may lead to expressive violence, or to an instrumental reliance on more forceful means of goal attainment (Marx 1990). For example, aggressive interdiction of youthful joy riders can bring about high-speed police chases that may end in extensive property damage, injury or death (Clarke and Harris 1992; Homel 1994). Increases in potential penalties may lead to more violent resistance to police at the time of arrest (Homel 1994). Other situations of police interaction with individual citizens or groups may entail reciprocal heightening of aggression—from dirty looks, to exchange of affront, to exchange of force. Overreaction or inept police intervention can grossly aggravate conditions that, if left to their own devices, would peter out or blow over. Creative policymaking and law enforcement require a good sense of when a situation requires benign neglect; where intervention is warranted, it should be delivered in a manner that minimises the potential for escalation (Veno and Veno 1993).

In some circumstances, the countermeasures in question may be unwittingly provocative. A recent insightful essay by Sherman (1993) notes that punishment may produce defiance, not deterrence, depending upon the recipient's perception of the fairness of the process by which it was delivered. Thus, while some individuals may be expected to respond to the threat or reality of punishment with compliance, others may evince a diametrically opposed reaction.

The same logic applies to business regulation. Bardach and Kagan (1982) recognized that "rulebook regulation" had a tendency to foster an organised culture of resistance in some businesspeople. In their recent work on nursing home regulation, Makkai and Braithwaite (1994) have found just such an effect, where in some contexts a deterrent regulatory posture actually *reduces* compliance.

Threatened restrictions or prohibitions of the sale of certain firearms may inspire increased purchases of such weapons in anticipation of future non-availability. The inspiration may extend to guns in general, thus leading to an overall increase in firearms ownership. The potency of the firearm as a symbol (negative for some, but positive for others) is such that proposals to regulate the ownership of weapons may trigger strong resistance.

In other circumstances, countermeasures may directly or indirectly lead to collateral damage of greater magnitude than that resulting from the target behaviour. Marx (1990) observed that fencing installed to discourage soccer hooliganism contributed to the deaths of 93 spectators who were crushed in the Hillsborough (U.K.) stadium disaster. He also noted that the casualty toll from the London Underground fire at Kings Cross was higher because of toxic fumes produced by chemicals contained in anti-graffiti paint. O'Malley (1994) noted that "speed humps" designed to slow vehicular traffic may occasion significant damage to vehicles (not to mention emergency vehicles) failing to reduce speed sufficiently.

Unintentional Enticement

It should come as no surprise to learn that warning messages may produce perverse effects. Merely by dramatising certain aspects of non-compliance, they can advertise the behaviour in question, bringing it to the attention of those who would otherwise be oblivious, or exciting the curiosity of those who would otherwise be only vaguely aware. Worse still, warning messages may entice the potentially rebellious. Symbolic protest is a common response to the moralistic injunction. Stern warnings from law enforcement authorities about the perils of various illicit drugs serve to publicise the substances in question in a manner that only the most creative minds in the advertising industry could hope to rival. Denunciation by moral entrepreneurs can impel the eager consumption of controversial literature, film and related material. The phenomenon in question, arguably both timeless and ubiquitous, has been termed the "forbidden fruit effect" (Sieber, 1981:136).

Reversal of Effects

Interventions may be seen to operate with intended effect in the short term, only to have their impact reverse over time. Sherman et al. (1991) observe that short-custody arrest for domestic violence, while producing a deterrent effect in the short term, actually produced a criminogenic or counter-deterrent effect for some groups with the passage of time.

A recent discussion of street lighting in Glasgow noted how an intervention introduced as a perceived solution can actually worsen the problem it was meant to address. To illustrate how feelings—and, indeed, the reality of safety—can be undermined rather than enhanced, one cannot improve upon the following words of one female respondent: "I think it's worse now: With the lights, people can see you. When they couldn't see you they didn't know who you were. You could be anybody. Now they can see you're a lassie" (quoted in Nair et al., 1993:560).

In his general discussion of counterproductive social interventions, Sieber (1981) suggests that situations can occur in which expectations may rise beyond the capacity of an intervention to meet them. In such circumstances, the effects of rebound may be worse than the status quo ante.

Labelling

One of the more popular theories in the sociology of deviance is that of labelling. Briefly stated, the designation of an individual as delinquent facilitates the internalization of that identity, increasing the likelihood of subsequent delinquent behaviour. The logic of labelling can be extended beyond offenders. One might suggest, for example, that to be labelled as a *victim* facilitates the internalization of that identity, and subtly reinforces a self-image of dependence and diminished autonomy. The result may be a prolongation of distress occasioned by the circumstances of victimization, and a delay of eventual recovery. Indeed, in some cases, labelling may entail a fatalistic resignation and repeated victimization. Perhaps for this reason, some advocates refer to the status as that of survivor rather than victim.

Labelling theory can have a spatial dimension as well. The mere identification of a place as dangerous or rowdy sends a signal. Persons who are risk-aversive and who value tranquility will be inclined to avoid such a location, while those who would be producers and consumers of risk would be attracted to such a place. Where signals of danger do not initially reflect empirical reality, they may operate as self-fulfilling prophecies, transforming both the image and the reality of a place. Of course, there are locations that are objectively unsafe or in the actual process of decline. To identify them otherwise could produce an unwarranted sense of security or, at best, incredulity. But absent visible indicia of deterioration, inappropriate crime prevention messages can "create" crime.

Warnings and Self-fulfilling Prophecies

We noted above how warning messages can be unintentionally enticing, thereby producing a "forbidden fruit effect." There are other ways in which warnings can become self-fulfilling. Those responsible for the regulation of banks and insurance companies are at times cautious about publicising the vulnerability of these financial institutions, lest the bad news trigger a run and bring about the very circumstances that regulators seek to prevent. Moral suasion and a hope that the beleaguered institution might trade out of its difficulties tends to be the preferred regulatory strategy.

Criminal Exploitation of Crime Prevention Information

Information can be a double-edged sword. On the one hand, it can be a useful instrument in the furtherance of risk reduction. On the other hand, crime prevention information may serve as instructional material in the methods of crime. There are circumstances in which information can be exploited in furtherance of precisely the activity it was intended to prevent. One need not be an expert in military strategy to recognize that knowledge of an adversary's defenses can be very helpful in planning an attack. So, too, with crime prevention.

When crime prevention entails nothing more than communicating ordinary criminal "street wisdom" to a wider public for purposes of target hardening, well and good. However, when the direction of information flow is reversed, and knowledge of vulnerabilities and countermeasures is communicated to prospective offenders, there is a risk that an otherwise criminally latent person may be tempted to try his or her hand, or that a person with more resolute criminal inclinations will exploit the information in order to adapt his or her modus operandi or otherwise circumvent the structures of prevention. Maintaining a degree of uncertainty can thus be an appropriate crime prevention strategy.

Under-enforcement

On the other hand, the existence of draconian sanctions may produce under-enforcement. This may reflect the tacit recognition that the "law on the books" defies practical application. The principle is as common to business regulation (Sunstein, 1990) as it is to those remaining laws that seek to regulate consensual sexual activity between adults in private. Overly restrictive laws encourage mutually dependent relations between nominal adversaries (Sieber, 1981). One hardly need mention the potential for corruption posed by certain types of prohibitions. Given the risks that would appear to beset under-enforcement and over-enforcement, it may be appropriate to think in terms of an optimal level of enforcement (Makkai and Braithwaite 1993; Viscusi and Zeckhauser, 1979).

Displacement

Perhaps the most familiar unintended consequence of crime prevention is displacement. The risk that undesirable activity, rather than prevented absolutely, will be shifted into other areas within or beyond one's jurisdiction or policy domain has become part of conventional criminological wisdom (Barr and Pease, 1990).

Depending upon the scope of analysis, one may envisage situations wherein displacement results in net loss. For example, criminality may be displaced from affluent, more resilient targets to those less able to afford loss. Clarke and Harris (1992) observe that new measures to prevent automobile theft will increase the vulnerability of older, cheaper vehicles. Alternatively, theft may be displaced to a location with more numerous and accessible targets. Distributive considerations aside, the risk inherent in displacement is that the displaced activity may have a more serious impact than the original activity, or that it might take a more intractable form.

Displacement is also evident in regulatory domains. The migration of industries to jurisdictions with relatively permissive regulatory regimes is often noted. The phenomena of cross-border and cross-media pollution are other examples (Guruswamy, 1991; Andrews, 1993). New smoke-stacks may improve British air quality, but only at the expense of Scandinavian forests and lakes damaged by acid rain. Within jurisdictions, the administration of tax laws is an ongoing drama involving authorities closing "loopholes," while a small industry exists to locate new avenues of avoidance and evasion.

Creative Adaptation

There are those crime prevention initiatives that may foreclose easy options, but in so doing inspire adaptive behaviour on the part of offenders that can entail more inventive, devious or violent activity. With a view to remaining "one step ahead of the law," entrepreneurial criminals may engage in increasingly refined avoidance behaviour. The ingenuity and adaptability of crime prevention targets may be enhanced by new challenges and, with repeated strengthening, may constitute a more formidable threat than was initially the case. Marx (1990) heralds an endless spiral of technologies and counter-technologies for crime and crime prevention.

This may entail the "professionalization" of crime. Marx (1981) observed how strict enforcement of drug laws can serve to neutralize opportunistic amateur dealers and thereby strengthen the market position of well-organized professionals. Supply reduction strategies that make for higher prices and higher profits can generate intense competition among drug dealers, which may manifest itself in energetic efforts to create new markets (Reuter and Kleiman, 1986; Sherman, 1992).

Adaptation may also characterise juvenile offending. Reiss (1980) and Klein (1993) have suggested that certain policies relating to juvenile gangs may have a counterproductive effect. The neutralization of a gang member through arrest may be followed by aggressive attempts to recruit a replacement. Such efforts may succeed so well that the size and cohesion of the gang would actually increase as a result.

Adaptation can at times be more brutal than creative. One could imagine, for example, an increase in hostage taking by robbers in response to physical security barriers in banks, or the threat of immolation by petrol rather than the use of firearms in the robbery of service station attendants protected by bullet-proof shields (Sherman 1992).

Technology may also be exploited to defeat law enforcement initiatives. The advent of radar detectors, CB radios and police-radio scanners has made traffic law enforcement that much more difficult (Kane 1993). Hidden speed cameras and aerial surveillance may, however, prove more difficult to circumvent.

Over-deterrence

In some cases, prevention measures or threatened sanctions may be so intense that they can have a detrimental effect on legitimate activity. Surveillance, for example, is often broad in scope and undiscriminating. The revolutions in information processing and surveillance technology have brought about a shrinking of one's private space, and have reduced the anonymity of public space. Crime prevention programs based on surveillance may achieve their goals, but in so doing may exert a chilling effect on public spontaneity. Programs that encourage citizens to report the sins of others may produce a deterrent effect, but may also create a society of informers in which no one can be trusted (Marx, 1989). Programs that require certain types of offenders, such as drunk drivers or child molesters, to identify themselves may invite harassment and vigilantism (Marx, 1990). Screening processes designed to prevent fraud against social welfare systems can be so rigorous that they exclude those who would be legitimate beneficiaries. Not only can they discourage legitimate claimants from seeking their entitlements, they may erroneously identify law-abiding persons as fraudulent (Marx, 1986).

Critics of business regulation often cite the threat of criminal liability as a disincentive to investment and innovation. It has recently been suggested that liability rules and prudential requirements in the U.S. have made responsible lenders overcautious, to the detriment of that nation's economic recovery (Rowlett, 1993). Downs (1973) observed that strict enforcement of building codes, ostensibly in the interests of the health and safety of low-income tenants, led to the abandonment of buildings by landlords and a consequent shortage of affordable accommodation.

Policies to discourage the employment of illegal immigrants may entail the threat of severe penalties for employers and strict liability for hiring workers without proper documentation. The strategy is at first blush compelling: not only would it appear to protect disadvantaged workers against exploitation by unscrupulous employers, it would serve to protect employment opportunities for legitimate members of the work force. In furtherance of these worthy ends, the state would enlist the resources of the employer in screening prospective employees.

To shift such potential risks and administrative burdens onto the employer may incline some to avoid employing members of ethnic minorities altogether. The price of discouraging the employment of illegal immigrants can thus be discrimination against immigrants in general.

A deterrent posture may be so ferocious that it defies credibility or even implementation. Sunstein (1990) reminds us that draconian standards may produce underregulation; regulators may be loath to enforce standards they perceive as too stringent, or to trigger penalties they perceive as too severe. The idea is hardly new; one may recall from the history of English criminal law the plethora of offences that carried the penalty of death, while only a relatively small proportion of crimes resulted in executions. Jurors and judges were simply reluctant to convict (Zimring and Hawkins 1973).

Perverse Incentives

Policies can be structured in such a manner as to provide perverse incentives, whether for the target of prevention activity or for third parties (Schultze, 1973). One need not be an economist to recognise that certain efforts in furtherance of prevention may distort markets in a manner that produces unforeseen, and often undesirable, outcomes.

During the 1993 Christmas season in the U.S., a well-meaning citizen sponsored a "toys-for-guns" program, whereby individuals could exchange a firearm for a gift certificate redeemable at a prominent chain of toy stores. The symbolism was so compelling that it captured the imagination of millions and inspired numerous variations on the "Gun Buyback" theme. Although the appeal of such strategies is considerable, and the reduction of a firearms inventory is doubtless laudable, it has been nevertheless suggested that such programs may distort the market for firearms, inadvertently subsidizing firearms manufacturers, possibly producing gun thefts, and enhancing the value of the least expensive weapons (Eckholm, 1994).

Interference in markets can produce singularly inappropriate incentives. Resort to theft in order to finance consumption of drugs is a pattern of behaviour deeply embedded in conventional criminological wisdom. Competition for drug markets often becomes violent. It should come as no surprise, therefore, that drug "crackdowns" may be accompanied by increases in violent crime (Sherman, 1992). In his study of police under-cover operations, Marx (1988) reminds us that police "stings" based on undercover purchase of stolen goods may serve to increase the number of active burglars. The threat of draconian penalties may also produce perverse incentives; the death penalty for murder will arguably place potential witnesses to any capital crime at greater risk of their lives. In those jurisdictions that impose capital punishment for offences other than homicide, the perpetrator may reduce the risk of execution by killing the victim outright.

Moral Hazard as an Incentive to Offend

The term "moral hazard" normally refers to the inclination of persons who are insured against a risk to engage in a greater degree of risk-taking activity (Heimer, 1985). Thus, persons who are insured against theft may be less likely to invest in additional security measures. But the term has been used more broadly to encompass incentives to offend. Consider policies whereby rewards are offered for citizen assistance in the detection and reporting of an offence (Levmore, 1986). The incentive to orchestrate an offence in order to claim an award for its detection or prosecution is hardly a novel idea. One imaginative practitioner who succeeded for a time was the celebrated eighteenth-century thief-taker Jonathan Wild (Howson, 1970). Until his arrangements were discovered, Wild practiced at two complementary professions. On the one hand, he would recover lost property for a commission; on the other, he operated simultaneously as a receiver of stolen goods. Such ironies are by no means limited to eighteenth-century property crime. Prior to a recent amendment, it was possible for the architect of a fraud against the U.S. government to seek a reward under the False Claims Act (Phillips, 1990).

Over and above issues of moral hazard, insurance generally is an invitation to fraud during periods of economic contraction or when the value of the insured asset has depreciated. Overinsurance, in particular, creates an ongoing incentive to destroy property (Heimer, 1985).

The domain of environmental protection provides other examples of perverse incentives. Consider, for example, a system of rebates for the return of toxic waste generated in a manufacturing process. In the absence of a carefully designed pricing structure, such a program might create incentives to increase the production of toxic waste. One could, for example, dilute a substance and seek a rebate for the larger volume. Alternatively, one could produce "counterfeit" waste, generating a substance for no other purpose than to claim a rebate (Russell, 1988). Landes and Posner (1975) have noted the incentive to breed noxious pests in order to claim a bounty for their extermination. Such a policy could produce the perverse effect of increasing the very problem which it was designed to address. It is, in effect, an invitation to fraud.

In addition to the risk of counterfeiting noted above, incentive systems, depending upon their structure, may invite collusion between prospective enforcers and offenders. Where the enforcer's potential reward is less than the offender's likely penalty, there exists an incentive for the prospective offender to bribe. Where the potential penalty is smaller than the potential reward, there is an incentive to fabricate an offence. A matter of greater concern arises when disincentives to prevent an offence are produced by the availability of greater compensation for disclosing an offence after the fact. An incentive thus exists to allow damage to occur in order to obtain a larger quantum of compensation (Landes and Posner, 1975).

Informers' reward programs also carry the potential for blackmail. A prospective informer may demand payment from a violator as a condition of refraining from disclosure. As long as the amount demanded is less than the expected costs (financial and non-material) that would flow from official knowledge of non-compliance, it will be in the violator's interest to pay "hush money."

Perhaps the most dramatic example of the moral hazard in recent regulatory affairs is the constellation of events collectively known as the savings and loan scandal that occurred in the U.S. during the latter half of the 1980s (Mayer, 1992). With a view toward stimulating the economy, the Reagan Administration relaxed prudential controls on small financial institutions, while at the same time insuring their deposits. The result could be described most charitably as a frenzy of unwise investment; in reality, a great deal of activity was sufficiently fraudulent as to give new meaning to the axiom "the easiest way to rob a bank is to own one."

Moral Hazard and Vulnerability to Victimization

Moral hazard more commonly refers to the propensity of persons insured against risk to engage in risk-taking behaviour. As knowledgeable insurance people are aware, the phenomenon of moral hazard has significant implications for crime prevention. For this reason, insurance contracts often have in-built conditions and incentives to undertake preventive measures.

Insurance aside, there are other occasions when moral hazard may operate to net disadvantage. These entail circumstances when prevention initiatives create a false sense of security. For example, it has been suggested that the use of "dummy" surveillance cameras may have a lulling effect on unwitting members of the public (Clarke and Weisburd, 1994). Police patrols with two officers may be more risk-prone than single officer patrols (Wilson and Brewer, 1992).

It has also been suggested that training in self-defence and assertiveness may enhance feelings of competence and self-esteem and, indeed, may enhance personal safety (McDaniel, 1993). While this may well be the case, such feelings may lead one to enter situations that are best avoided, and perhaps may contribute to the escalation of violence (Skogan and Block, 1986). A spouse's new-found assertiveness may be viewed by a chronically abusive partner as provocative and as justification for further abuse (O'Leary et al., 1985; Black, 1984). In his study of high-speed police pursuits, Homel (1990) reported that police officers with advanced driver training tended to have more accidents than their counterparts without such training.

One of the more interesting debates in recent years surrounds the deterrent consequences of the private ownership of firearms. While some have argued that a significant amount of crime is deterred by the realization that the prospective victim may be armed (Kleck, 1988; Kleck and Patterson, 1993), advocates of firearms control argue that arming in self-defence will contribute to firearms accidents, escalation of violence between victim and offender, and opportunistic use of firearms in interpersonal disputes (Kellermann, 1993, 1992; Cook, 1993; Zimring, 1991).

Crime Prevention as Fear Generation

We have seen above how crime prevention activity can produce a false sense of security, and may lead to unwarranted risk-taking. The flip side of this would entail situations in which crime prevention initiatives generate a degree of fear, cynicism and suspicion unwarranted by empirical reality (Marx, 1986). Rather than enhancing freedom, some technologies of crime prevention may produce a fortress mentality (O'Malley, 1992). While one of the fundamental objectives of crime prevention is fear reduction, there remains the risk that crime prevention activity may actually exacerbate fear of crime (Rosenbaum, 1988; Rosenbaum et al., 1986; Winkel, 1991). A recent longitudinal study reported a positive relationship between precautionary behaviours and fear of crime (Norris and Kaniasty, 1992). Various child protection programs have been criticised for delivering more fear than actual security.

The above review of the many ways in which crime prevention efforts can produce harm is almost certainly not exhaustive, nor are the types mutually exclusive. Barr and Pease (1990), for example, observe that displacement can entail escalation. Our task now is to begin to understand how the "best laid plans" can so easily go astray.

PART THREE: EXPLAINING COUNTERPRODUCTIVE CRIME PREVENTION

The most cynical explanation of counterproductive crime prevention would hold that authorities are less focused on longer-term realities than they are with short-term image. In such a world, crime prevention programs exist not so much to prevent crime as to demonstrate official concern and the illusion of action. Ultimate outcomes, if less than successful, are likely to be someone else's problem. Whether or not this may be an intractable fact of life in contemporary Western democratic political systems cannot distract us too greatly for present purposes. We may not be able to lengthen the periodicity of electoral cycles, but we can at least acknowledge—and indeed celebrate—the contributions of true policy visionaries. In any event, for those who may be involved in the actual engineering of crime prevention programs, there are more scientifically significant considerations. We turn now to a practical discussion of what might be termed "engineering flaws" in the design and implementation of crime prevention programs.

Bad Science

Wishful thinking is no substitute for theoretical understanding. Underlying most crime prevention failures, ironic or otherwise, is bad science. In this regard, perhaps the most common pitfall is the tendency to overgeneralize. General theory may be the ideal of scientists, but inappropriate application of general theory, or failure to account for situational variation, can be the bane of those who might seek to make a difference in the real world (Braithwaite, 1993). What works in Wollongong might fail on Palm Island.

Even in a limited setting, those policy entrepreneurs who are enamoured of a certain paradigm, such as rational choice or deterrence theory, may discover that not all targets of control are "utility maximizers." Some targets, in fact, may act in a very irrational manner. The threat of punishment may *invite* offending. We can learn about human behaviour from the Imp of Perversity as well as from James Buchanan. Recall how the identical stimulus can elicit compliance from some individuals, and provoke defiance on the part of others.

The same risks may beset those who would prevent and control corporate crime. As Fisse and Braithwaite (1993) remind us, "organizations are so different that any universalistic approach to controlling them will encounter difficulty" (p. 130). So it is that the cutting edge of corporate criminology envisages the ideal regulatory policy as entailing a mix of instruments best-suited for specific organizational contexts (Gunningham, 1993).

It is often tempting to generalize from past policy outcomes that have met with apparent success. Closer examination, whether through replication or secondary analysis, may reveal nuances not previously apparent that can seriously limit the generalizability of findings. One recalls, for example, the widely heralded findings from Minneapolis on the deterrent effects of mandatory arrest for spouse abuse. Because of the apparent operational success of this form of intervention, as well as its intuitive appeal and resonance with the retributive inclinations of many of those concerned over the problem of spouse abuse, its adoption was widely advocated (Sherman and Cohn, 1989). Only later did it become apparent that the intervention of mandatory arrest was effective in preventing recidivism by some abusive spouses and not others. Specifically, Sherman (1993) found an interaction effect between arrest and unemployment; arrestees who were employed were less likely to reoffend, but unemployed arrestees were *more* likely to do so.

Another potential source of ironic reversal, and of crime prevention failure in general, is the tendency to intervene at an inappropriate point in the causal chain that produces the problem in question. The practice of treating the symptoms of a problem rather than its causes is as risk-prone as it is familiar (Marx, 1990); post-hoc nuisance abatement is no substitute for prevention (Janicke 1990). The aforementioned anecdote about improving the lighting in the Glasgow neighbourhood is a good example.

A more basic scientific shortcoming is the apparent failure to understand the causal processes upon which one seeks to intervene. Recall the observations of Sherman (1993) that a deterrent stimulus perceived as fair will have its intended effect, while the identical stimulus—if perceived as unjust—will elicit defiance and resistance. An invitation to empathy will have no impact upon the affectless; the spectre of shame no effect upon the shameless.

Moreover, there remains the possibility that an intervention can trigger other causal processes. The functional disruption of related systems is familiar to students of ecology. Similar principles apply in social life (Sieber, 1981). McCord's (1978) follow-up analysis of the Cambridge-Somerville program suggests possible reasons for that program's ironic outcomes. She observes that contact with program staff whose values differed from those of the participants' own families may have produced conflicts that produced subsequent dissatisfaction. Assistance and support provided by the program may have engendered dependency and expectations on the part of participants. These expectations, when unfulfilled following conclusion of the program, may have created resentment. The warm inner glow of benevolence may have prevented program designers from anticipating that their interventions would generate such consequential side effects.

In addition to inadequate understanding of basic causal processes, there is often among policy entrepreneurs an inadequate appreciation of the systemic nature of modern society. Given the density of contemporary social space, efforts to influence one variable are likely to influence others, either directly or indirectly. Engineers of crime prevention are often insufficiently aware of the wider social ecology—the complex, interdependent systems of social life in which the target behaviour resides. Most policies have wider ramifications.

Two facts of life compound this situation. The first is a common inclination to oversimplify problems and their solutions, a phenomenon too familiar to dwell upon here. Another is the bureaucratic specialization that characterises contemporary public administration. Not only does this produce a degree of professional tunnel vision, it creates a risk that parochial organizational goals may dilute or displace the main thrust of the intervention.

The fragmented nature of much policy space means that decisions taken in one policy sphere often have impacts in others. The movement to deinstitutionalize mental hospital patients in the 1970s and 1980s was heralded as humane and progressive; life in "the community" simply had to be better than in the Dickensian institutions of the state. The absence of intermediate care or community-based facilities, however, resulted in new problems of public order and homelessness, with a substantial increase in the workload of police, welfare, and housing authorities.

Bad Planning

Ironic policy reversals may also result from bad planning. One of the most fundamental causes of bad planning is the failure to learn. Learning failures may take a variety of forms. One can, of course, be genuinely ignorant of precedent—oblivious to the past. But dissonance reduction is a more common human characteristic; it is much more common to luxuriate in one's previous triumphs than to dwell on one's past blunders. Unfortunate episodes of the past are more often repressed, their inherent lessons unlearned.

Although many organizations lack the institutional memory to assist in planning, numerous models exist. Principles of aviation and maritime safety have developed systematically in response to accidents. The cumulative wisdom that they represent make it all that much more difficult to repeat a course of action that has previously had disastrous consequences.

These problems are compounded by some common principles of the sociology of knowledge. Those who may be unable to forget their past mistakes are nevertheless unlikely to flaunt them. Planning failures, not to mention planning disasters, are not usually publicised, and are even less likely to find their way into the scientific literature.

Sieber (1981) suggests a number of manifestations of bad planning. The time required to achieve program goals may be greater than originally anticipated. Planners may underestimate the scope and depth of the target problem, as well as the quantity and quality of the intervention required to successfully address it. Thus, many short-term gains lead ultimately to defeat.

Implementation Failure

A final source of counterproductive crime prevention arises from defects in program implementation. This can entail resource inadequacy, lack of coordination between the various interests involved, and failure of oversight.

Resource Inadequacy

Programs that might otherwise succeed can fail because of a lack of resources. The program itself may be well-conceived and on target, but may founder because the intervention is of insufficient strength to affect on the problem. To use an analogy, where a sufficient dose of antibiotics can combat an infection, an insufficient dose may in fact aggravate the disease. Just as infrastructure maintenance deferred in order to save money may result ultimately in greater costs, so too can half-hearted investment in a program lead to failure and the necessity of greater remedial expenditures down the track.

Perhaps on a more mundane level is the suggestion that effective employment of security guards (or indeed, public police) requires that they be sufficiently compensated to offset the temptation to take advantage of the criminal opportunities open to them. In the absence of an appropriate incentive structure, these temptations can become part of the problem. Elsewhere, Clarke and his collaborators (1994) report how the initial design of new coin collection machines for the London Underground was of insufficient sophistication to prevent the use of slugs. Following widespread exploitation of the design shortcomings, authorities were forced to reinvest in more complex (and expensive) technology.

Lack of Coordination

The complexities of public policy often entail the involvement of more than one organization. Implementation failure may occur because of insufficient coordination between agencies with responsibility for or influence upon a program. There may be conflict and inconsistencies within and between relevant agencies; organizations can operate at cross-purposes (Castellani, 1992). The unfortunate consequence of the deinstitutionalization of the mentally ill was noted above. Policy analysts generally would do well to focus on the overlap of policy space during program development and implementation. Bottoms and Wiles (1988), for example, discuss the relationship between crime and housing policy.

In the best of all possible worlds, interagency coordination would be natural and flawless. But in the real world, where institutional fragmentation tends to be the rule, organizations often have their own agendas and priorities (Robertson, 1989). The risk that program goals will be displaced by organizational imperatives will increase with the number of agencies involved.

Oversight Failure

Another factor contributing to counterproductive crime prevention is lack of monitoring and oversight. For those concerned with image rather than substance, this may be of less concern. But for those seeking to effect genuine change, some kind of monitoring system is essential. Just as one should take care in generalizing from successful crime prevention outcomes, so too should one beware of overgeneralizing from crime prevention failures. The fact that a particular program is found to have negative consequences does not necessarily imply that the type of intervention in general is counterproductive; rather, it may be inhibitive only as specifically configured.

Some failures develop slowly enough to be noticed before causing irreparable damage, and corrective measures may be taken. However, there often exists the disinclination to perceive indicia of failure when they begin to appear. The tendency to perceive favourable evidence and to minimize disconfirming evidence is particularly strong on the part of those who may have a vested interest in program success (Chan, 1979).

Table 1 summarizes the above discussion by suggesting the salience of the explanatory factors for each type of regressive outcome. Situational

Table 1: Regressive Crime Prevention Outcomes and their Explanation

	Scientific Inadequacy		Planning Failure	Implementation Deficits		
	Over Generalization	Poor Causal Analysis		Resources	Coordination	Oversight
ESCALATION	✔	✔	✔			✔
Enticement	✔		✔			
Reversal of Effects		✔		✔		✔
Labelling		✔				✔
Self-fulfilling Prophecy		✔	✔			
Criminal Exploitation						
Under-enforcement			✔	✔		✔
DISPLACEMENT		✔		✔		
CREATIVE ADAPTATION		✔	✔			
OVER-DETERRENCE			✔		✔	
PERVERSE INCENTIVES		✔	✔		✔	
Fear generation			✔			

prevention activities would appear most vulnerable to displacement, creative adaptation and overdeterrence. These regressive outcomes are most likely to arise from deficits in planning and coordination. Social crime prevention initiatives, by contrast, appear at risk of resulting in escalation. This risk appears to arise primarily from inadequate scientific analysis, reinforced by shortcomings in planning. The hypotheses implicit in Table 1 must at this stage be regarded as tentative. One hopes they are amenable to testing and refinement by subsequent analysis.

PART FOUR: REDUCING THE RISK OF COUNTERPRODUCTIVE CRIME PREVENTION

At this stage, it would be delightful to deliver a revolutionary new recipe for fail-safe crime prevention policy. Unfortunately, nothing remotely resembling such an alluring prospect is at hand. Rather, and somewhat anticlimactically, what are available are some basic principles derived largely from common sense. Their saving virtue is that they can be ignored only at one's peril.

There is an important role for evangelists in crime prevention. Political mobilization and marketing are essential to the crime prevention enterprise, and evangelists are better at these tasks than are skeptics. Skeptics, too, play an essential role: as they never tire of reminding us, many roads to disaster are paved with the best of intentions. A less visible, but no less important, role is that of analyst. An effective crime prevention program will probably require the efforts of all three.

Analysis

First, crime prevention planners should make an effort to understand the context and mechanisms of their intended activity. They should comprehend the systems in which they propose to intervene, and the processes they propose to disrupt. They should look beyond the superficial, mechanistic doctrines of opportunity and deterrence, and understand the psychological processes, social organization, and economic systems in which target behaviour is embedded (Felson, 1994).

These systems can be as diverse as the mind-set of homeless Aboriginal youths, the social network of an ethnic street gang, or the market for heroin in a given region. Given the density of policy space, planners should also attend to the political and administrative systems on which their programs will impinge (Castellani, 1992). A grounding in principles of ecology and systems thinking will be useful in this regard. Those who design crime prevention programs would do well to engage in "pluralist planning" (Chan, 1979), and devise scenarios from a variety of institutional perspectives (Hall, 1980). They should invite independent analytical criticism and the search for likely interactions that may be overlooked by a program's designers. One might suggest an ongoing role for the institutionalized skeptic, one whose role it is to pose hard questions.

To the extent possible, planners should endeavour to model a proposed intervention and anticipate the ramifications of their program, especially the program's potential downside risks. Planners should then seek to structure their intervention in a manner that would minimise the negative externalities in question. An outstanding example of research that consciously sought to anticipate various systemic impacts of a prospective policy intervention is the feasibility research into the controlled availability of opioids, conducted at the Australian National University's National Centre for Epidemiology and Population Health. This project sought to identify a wide range of repercussions that might arise in the event that heroin were distributed on a controlled basis to dependent persons in the Australian Capital Territory. For example, Bammer and her colleagues sought, among other things, to assess public opinion regarding the controlled distribution of heroin; the effect which such a distribution scheme would have on the existing illicit market; and means of reducing the risk that such a policy would attract drug users to Canberra from other parts of Australia.

Special care should be taken in the design of crime prevention protocols. Recall McCord's (1978) suggestion that the delivery of services in the Cambridge-Somerville Program may have unwittingly generated tensions in the treatment recipients. Also recall Winkel's (1991) finding that the form in which crime prevention information is communicated can spell either success or increased insecurity. Negative communication strategies can enhance fear of crime without reducing risk.

The risk of being blinded by public pressure for a quick fix is a common feature of contemporary politics. The tendency to be dazzled by a particular technology or method may lead to its overuse and eventually to its diminishing effectiveness. Interventions with particular symbolic value or resonance, such as "boot camps" for juvenile offenders, "toys-for-guns" programs, or mandatory sentencing structures based on the principle of "three strikes and you're out," should not be embraced uncritically.

Anticipatory planning is central to policy development (Pressman and Wildavsky, 1984). One hardly needs reminding that large-scale interventions are best undertaken only after piloting or pre-testing. But while they are in operation, crime prevention initiatives—or, indeed, pilot studies—should incorporate built-in feedback mechanisms, monitoring systems and contingency plans in the event that negative consequences start to become apparent (Sieber, 1981; Pressman and Wildavsky, 1984). Early warning of dysfunction may permit refinement or modification. The need for such contingency planning should be obvious in projects like the Kansas City Preventive Patrol Experiment, where preventive patrols were withdrawn from randomly selected areas of the city without informing residents. Kelling (1985) describes how the experimental procedures provided for monitoring of crime rates over the course of the experiment and contingency plans to terminate the project in the event of unacceptable increases in crime. Of course, interventions whose effects may not become apparent until after the significant passage of time are less amenable to corrective feedback. Recall the Cambridge-Somerville study, where the adverse impact on participants' mortality was not evident for many years.

Ethics

The risk that even successful crime prevention initiatives may cause collateral harm suggests that those who would design prevention programs adhere to the highest ethical standards. Even the probability of laudable ends may not justify the means. Very few interventions would appear to be entirely risk-free. Those who design and implement crime prevention policy should anticipate the risks faced by subjects and by third parties, and do their best to ensure that their likely distribution is equitable and that they do not outweigh the benefits of the proposed intervention. In particular, they should be attuned to existing incentive structures and systems of informal social control, and seek to envisage how their proposed intervention might affect them (Grasmick and Bursik, 1990). Where the intervention will have an impact on a market, an attempt should be made to anticipate what that impact will entail.

One could perhaps be excused for concluding from the above discussion that nothing works, nothing can be made to work, and any efforts to this end will only produce more harm than good. But this is not the case. The intended message was rather that rigorous policy analysis is an essential ingredient of crime prevention, and that there is a role for institutionalized skepticism (as opposed to cynicism) in the crime prevention enterprise. Just as knowledge advances through negative findings, so too can policy.

The majority of those with an interest in crime prevention would regard it as the most productive approach to the problem of crime that confronts contemporary society. As such, they might tend to regard it uncritically. The disinclination or unwillingness to recognise potential harm is common.

All innovation entails a degree of risk. The challenge for crime prevention is to contain that risk within reasonable limits. Just as engineering failures can be the basis of subsequent design successes (Petroski, 1985) so, too, can the analysis of counterproductive crime prevention activity be instructive.

It has become trite to quote Santayana's dictum that those who cannot remember the past are condemned to repeat it. But one can learn a great deal from disappointment. Failure analysis is central to the profession of engineering; so too should it become central to the professions of crime prevention and criminal justice.

Acknowledgements: Thanks are due Janine Bush, for research assistance; and John Braithwaite, Ron Clarke, Ross Homel, Gloria Laycock, and Heather Strang, for helpful advice.

NOTES

1. This refers to correctional practices which may increase the risk of recidivism. Reference to prisons as "schools of crime" are as old as prisons themselves; authorities in many jurisdictions will concede that few people leave prison as more able to function as responsible citizens than when they entered. (See generally: Hawkins, 1976, Chapter 3.)

2. One cheerfully notes the contributions of Clarke and Weisburd (1994), who report a variety of positive unintended consequences of crime prevention activities.

3. These exclude crimes committed by agencies of criminal justice. (See: Grabosky, 1989; Marx, 1988.)

4. Marx (1981) also discusses the criminogenic consequences of *non-enforcement* and *covert facilitation*. For comprehensive discussions of the latter, see Marx, 1988, and the symposium published in the *Journal of Social Issues* 1987 43(3).

5. Makkai and Braithwaite (1994) identify the personality trait of emotionality as likely to provide the basis of a defiant response to a deterrent regulatory posture, especially when regulatory enforcement is perceived as mistrustful and challenging to one's professionalism.

6. For discussions of labelling theory, see: Braithwaite, (1989, 16-20); Farrington, Ohlin and Wilson (1986, 111-19).

7. For discussions of repeated or multiple victimization experiences, see: Meier and Miethe (1993) and Sparks (1981).

8. The phenomenon of neighbourhood decline is evocatively discussed by Wilson and Kelling (1982) and Skogan (1990).

9. Of course, the causal ordering of this relationship may be reversed. Authorities, with no intention of enforcing the letter of the law, may increase penalties for symbolic purposes. One finds in the realm of business regulation, for example, relatively harsh penalties on the books but relatively gentle enforcement and sanctioning (Grabosky and Braithwaite, 1986). Cynics could perhaps be excused for speculating that this is precisely what authorities intended.

10. As Barr and Pease (1990) suggest, displacement may occur in a number of dimensions. It may occur over time or across space; it may entail a shift in targets, methods or offence types. It should be noted that displacement, far from being an unintended consequence of crime prevention activity, may actually be a goal. There are those who concede the inevitability of undesirable activity, and are simply concerned that it not occur "on their watch" or in their "backyard."

11. There are those who suggest that the justice system is inherently biased against disadvantaged minorities, and that forces as inevitable as gravity

will militate against them (Black, 1989). Displacement in general will be regressively redistributive.

12. It is said that years ago, so rigorous was the surveillance of public lavatories by plainclothes police that the New South Wales Teachers' Federation warned its members, regardless of sexual preference, to avoid using such facilities in Sydney lest they run the risk of being charged with intent to engage in what was then illicit sexual activity. On a less dramatic note, Marx (1990) has observed that the removal of seating facilities in public places to discourage loitering serves to deny everyone a place to sit.

13. Other authorities argue, to the contrary, that stringent regulation can provide the impetus for innovation and thereby enhance competitive advantage (see Porter, 1990). As we noted above in the discussion of escalation, new challenges may inspire criminals to engage in creative adaptation.

14. Gloria Laycock (personal communication, May 1995) related the tale of two British ladies on the beach in Spain, who saw a young Spanish boy treating an injured bird as a football. The lady was appalled, and paid the child to give the bird to her so that she could take it away and care for it. She was alarmed to find, therefore, a few hours later, a queue of young Spanish boys at her door, all holding injured birds, and all asking for payment.

15. The vigor of the debate may be explained in part by the likelihood that there is an element of truth to the position taken by each side.

16. For the classic statement of public choice theory, see Buchanan and Tulloch (1962). For a wider overview, see Caporaso and Levine (1992).

17. A recent observer of policy failures in general criticises the tendency of governments to focus their attention too far down the chain of causation, where problems and interventions are most visible. (See Janicke, 1990, chapter 3.)

18. For a discussion of the adverse impact of inflated expectations, see Boudon (1982).

19. One need only recall how the deinstitutionalization of the mentally ill affected not only on health systems, but also on housing, welfare, and law enforcement.

20. One might also wish to maximize the diffusion of crime control benefits (see note 3 *supra*).

21. See Bammer (1993); Bammer et al., (1994a); Bammer et al., (1994b).

REFERENCES

Andrews, R. (1993). "Long Range Planning in Environmental and Health Regulation." _Ecology Law Quarterly_ 20(3):515-582.

Bammer, G. (1993). "Should The Controlled Provision of Heroin Be a Treatment Option? Australian Feasibility Considerations." _Addiction_ 88:467-475.

—— D. Tunnicliff, and D. Chadwick-Masters (1994). _How Could an Influx of Users be Prevented if Canberra Introduces a Trial of Controlled Availability of Heroin?_ Working Paper No. 9, Feasibility Research into the Controlled Availability of Opioids. Canberra, AUS: National Centre for Epidemiology and Population Health, Australian National University.

—— and A. Sengoz (1994b). _How Would the Controlled Availability of Heroin Affect the Illicit Market in the Australian Capital Territory? An Examination of the Structure of the Illicit Heroin Market and Methods to Measure Changes in Price, Purity and Availability, Including Heroin Related Overdoses._ Working Paper No. 10, Feasibility Research into the Controlled Availability of Opioids. Canberra, AUS: National Centre for Epidemiology and Population Health, Australian National University.

Bardach, E. and R. Kagan (1982). _Going by the Book: The Problem of Regulatory Unreasonableness._ Philadelphia, PA: Temple University Press.

Barr, R. and K. Pease (1990). "Crime Placement, Displacement and Deflection." In: M. Tonry and N. Morris (eds.), _Crime and Justice: An Annual Review of Research_, vol. 12. Chicago, IL: University of Chicago Press.

Black, D. (1984). "Crime as Social Control." In: D. Black (ed.) _Toward a General Theory of Social Control_, vol 2. Orlando, FL: Academic Press.

—— (1989). _Sociological Justice._ New York, NY: Oxford University Press

Bottoms, A. and P. Wiles (1988). "Crime and Housing Policy: A Framework for Crime Prevention Analysis." In: T. Hope and M. Shaw (eds.), _Communities and Crime Reduction._ London, UK: Her Majesty's Stationery Office.

Boudon, R. (1982). _The Unintended Consequences of Social Action._ New York, NY: St Martin's Press.

Braithwaite, J. (1989). _Crime Shame and Reintegration._ New York, NY: Cambridge University Press.

—— (1993). "Beyond Positivism: Learning From Contextual Integrated Strategies." *Journal of Research in Crime and Delinquency* 30(4):383-399.

Buchanan, J. and G. Tulloch (1962). *The Calculus of Consent*. Ann Arbor, MI: University of Michigan Press.

Caporaso, J. and D. Levine (1992). *Theories of Political Economy*. New York, NY: Cambridge University Press.

Castellani, P. (1992). "Closing Institutions in New York State: Implementation and Management Lessons." *Journal of Policy Analysis and Management* 11(4):593-611.

Chan, S. (1979). "The Intelligence of Stupidity: Understanding Failures in Strategic Warning." *American Political Science Review* 73(1):171-80.

Clarke, R.V., R.P. Cody, and M. Natarajan (1994). "Subway Slugs: Tracking Displacement on the London Underground." *British Journal of Criminology* 34(2):122-138.

—— and P. Harris (1992). "Auto Theft and Its Prevention." In: M. Tonry (ed.), *Crime and Justice: A Review of Research*, vol.16. Chicago, IL: University of Chicago Press.

—— and D. Weisburd (1994). "Diffusion of Crime Control Benefits: Observations on the Reverse of Displacement." In: R.V. Clarke (ed.), *Crime Prevention Studies*, vol. 2. Monsey, NY: Criminal Justice Press.

Cook, P. (1993). "Notes on the Availability and Prevalence of Firearms." *American Journal of Preventive Medicine*, 9(3):33-38.

Downs, A. (1973). "Evaluating Efficiency and Equity in Federal Urban Programs." In: R. Haveman and R. Hamrin (eds.), *The Political Economy of Federal Policy*. New York, NY: Harper & Row.

Eckholm, E. (1994). "Add Gun Buybacks to the Public Wish List." *New York Times*, January 4, p. E4.

Farrington, D., L. Ohlin and J. Wilson (1986). *Understanding and Controlling Crime: Toward a New Strategy*. New York, NY: Springer-Verlag.

Felson, M. (1994). *Crime and Everyday Life: Insight and Implications for Society*. Thousand Oaks, CA: Pine Forge Press.

Fisse, B. and J. Braithwaite (1993). *Corporations, Crime and Accountability*. Cambridge, UK: Cambridge University Press.

Grabosky, P. (1989). *Wayward Governance: Illegality and its Control in the Public Sector*. Canberra, AUS: Australian Institute of Criminology.

—— and J. Braithwaite (1986). *Of Manners Gentle: Enforcement Strategies of Australian Business Regulatory Agencies*. Melbourne, AUS: Oxford University Press.

Grasmick, H. and R. Bursik (1990). "Conscience, Significant Others and Rational Choice: Extending the Deterrence Model." *Law and Society Review* 24:837-61.

Gunningham, N. (1993). "Thinking About Regulatory Mix—Regulating Occupational Health and Safety, Futures Markets and Environmental Law." In: P. Grabosky and J. Braithwaite (eds.) *Business Regulation and Australia's Future.* Canberra, AUS: Australian Institute of Criminology.

Guruswamy, L. (1991). "The Case for Integrated Pollution Control." *Law and Contemporary Problems* 54(4):41-56.

Hall, P. (1980). *Great Planning Disasters.* London, UK: Weidenfeld and Nicholson.

Hawkins, G. (1976). *The Prison: Policy and Practice.* Chicago, IL: University of Chicago Press.

Heimer, C. (1985). *Reactive Risk and Rational Action: Managing Moral Hazard in Insurance Contracts.* Berkeley, CA: University of California Press.

Homel, R. (1990). *High Speed Police Pursuits in Perth: A Report to the Police Department of Western Australia.* Perth, WA: Western Australia Police Department.

—— (1994). *Flawed Order: The Administration of Justice in a "Get Tough" Era.* (Inaugural Lecture.) Faculty of Education, Griffith University, Queensland, AUS.

Howson, G. (1970). *Thief-Taker General: The Rise and Fall of Jonathan Wild.* London, UK: Hutchinson.

Janicke, M. (1990). *State Failure: The Impotence of Politics in Industrial Society.* Cambridge, UK: Polity Press.

Kane, E. (1993). "Reflexive Adaptation." *Law and Policy* 15(3):179-90.

Kellermann, A. (1992). "Suicide in the Home in Relation to Gun Ownership." *New England Journal of Medicine* 327(7):467-472.

—— (1993). "Gun Ownership as a Risk Factor for Homicide in the Home." *New England Journal of Medicine* 329(15):1084-1091.

Kelling, G. (1985). "Justifying the Moral Propriety of Experimentation: A Case Study." In: W. Gellner (ed.), *Police Leadership in America.* New York, NY: Praeger.

Kleck, G. (1988). "Crime Control Through the Private Use of Armed Force." *Social Problems* 35:1-21.

—— and B. Patterson (1992). "The Impact of Gun Control and Gun Ownership Levels on Violence Rates." *Journal of Quantitative Criminology* 9(3):289-307.

Klein, M. (1993). "Attempting Crime Control by Suppression: The Misuse of Deterrence Principles." In: *Studies in Crime and Crime Prevention,* 2:88-112.

Landes, W. and R. Posner (1975). "The Private Enforcement of Law." *Journal of Legal Studies* 4(1):1-46.

Levmore, S. (1986). "Waiting for Rescue: An Essay on the Evolution and Incentive Structure of the Law of Affirmative Obligations." *Virginia Law Review* 72(5):879-941.

Makkai, T. and J. Braithwaite (1993). "The Limits of the Economic Analysis of Regulation: An Empirical Case and a Case for Empiricism." *Law and Policy* 15(4):271-291.

—— and J. Braithwaite (1994). "The Dialectics of Corporate Deterrence." *Journal of Research in Crime and Delinquency* 31(4):347-373.

Marx, G.T. (1981). "Ironies of Social Control: Authorities as Contributors to Deviance Through Escalation, Nonenforcement, and Covert Facilitation." *Social Problems* 28(3):221-246.

—— (1986). "The Iron Fist and the Velvet Glove: Totalitarian Potentials Within Democratic Structures." In: J. Short (ed.), *The Social Fabric: Dimensions and Issues.* Beverly Hills, CA: Sage.

—— (1988). *Undercover: Police Surveillance in America.* Berkeley, CA: University of California Press.

—— (1989). "Commentary: Some Trends and Issues in Citizen Involvement in the Law Enforcement Process." *Crime & Delinquency*, 35(3):500-519.

—— (1990). "The Engineering of Social Control: The Search for the Silver Bullet." Unpublished manuscript, Massachusetts Institute of Technology, Cambridge, MA.

Mayer, M. (1992). *The Greatest Ever Bank Robbery: The Collapse of the Savings and Loan Industry.* New York, NY: Collier Books.

McCord, J. (1978). "A Thirty-Year Follow-up of Treatment Effects." *American Psychologist* (March):284-89.

Mc Daniel, P. (1993). "Self Defence Training and Women's Fear of Crime." *Women's Studies International Forum* 16(1):37-45.

Meier, R.F. and T. Miethe (1993). "Understanding Theories of Criminal Victimization." In: M. Tonry (ed.) *Crime and Justice: A Review of Research*, vol. 17. Chicago, IL: University of Chicago Press.

Nair, G., J. Ditton and S. Phillips, Samuel (1993). "Environmental Improvements and Fear of Crime: The Sad Case of the 'Pond' Area in Glasgow." *British Journal of Criminology* 33(4):555-61.

Norris, F. and K. Kaniasty (1992). "A Longitudinal Study of the Effects of Various Crime Prevention Strategies on Criminal Victimization, Fear of Crime, and Psychological Distress." *American Journal of Community Psychology* 20(5):625-648.

O'Leary, D., A. Curley, A. Rosenbaum and C. Clarke (1985). "Assertion Training for Abused Wives: A Potentially Hazardous Treatment." *Journal of Marriage and Family Therapy* 11:319-22.

O'Malley, P. (1992). "Risk, Power and Crime Prevention." *Economy and Society* 21(3):252-275.

—— (1994). "Neo-Liberal Crime Control: Political Agendas and the Future of Crime Prevention in Australia." In: D. Chappell and P. Wilson (eds.) _The Australian Criminal Justice System: The Mid 1990's._ Sydney, AUS: Butterworths.

Petroski, H. (1985). _To Engineer is Human: The Role of Failure in Successful Design._ New York, NY: St. Martin's Press.

Phillips, J. (1990). Testimony before the Subcommittee on Administrative Law and Governmental Relations, Committee on the Judiciary, U.S. House of Representatives, April 4. Washington, DC: U.S. Government Printing Office.

Porter, M. (1990). _The Competitive Advantage of Nations._ London, UK: Macmillan.

Pressman, J. and A. Wildavsky (1984). _Implementation,_ 3d ed. Berkeley, CA: University of California Press.

Reiss, A.J., Jr. (1980). "Understanding Changes in Crime Rates." In: S. Feinberg and A. J. Reiss, Jr. (eds.) _Indicators of Crime and Criminal Justice: Quantitative Studies._ Washington, DC: U.S. Government Printing Office.

Reuter, P. and M. Kleiman (1986). "Risks and Prices: An Economic Analysis of Drug Enforcement." In: M. Tonry and N. Morris (eds.) _Crime and Justice: An Annual Review of Research,_ Vol. 7. Chicago, IL: University of Chicago Press.

Robertson, D. (1989). "Planned Incapacity to Succeed? Policy Structure and Social Policy Failure." _Policy Studies Review_ 8(2):241-63.

Rosenbaum, D. (1988). "A Critical Eye on Neighbourhood Watch: Does it Reduce Crime and Fear?" In: T. Hope and M. Shaw (eds.), _Communities and Crime Reduction._ London. UK: Her Majesty's Stationery Office.

—— D. Lewis, A. Grant (1986). "Neighbourhood-Based Crime Prevention in Chicago: A Look at the Impact of Community Organizing." In: D. Rosenbaum (ed.), _Community Crime Prevention: Does it Work?_ Beverly Hills, CA: Sage.

Rowlett, J. (1993). "The Chilling Effect of the Financial Institutions Reform, Recovery and Enforcement Act of 1989 and the Bank Fraud Prosecution Act of 1990: Has Congress Gone Too Far?" _American Journal of Criminal Law_ 20(2):239-262.

Russell, C. (1988). "Economic Incentives in the Management of Hazardous Wastes." _Columbia Journal of Environmental Law_ 13:257-274.

Schultze, C. (1973). " Perverse Incentives and the Inefficiency of Government." In: Haveman and Hamrin (eds.), _The Political Economy of Federal Policy._ New York, NY: Harper & Row.

Sherman, L. (1992). "Attacking Crime: Police and Crime Control." In: M. Tonry and N. Morris (eds.) _Crime and Justice: A Review of Research,_ vol. 15. Chicago, IL: University of Chicago Press.

—— (1993). "Defiance, Deterrence and Irrelevance: A Theory of the Criminal Sanction." *Journal of Research in Crime and Delinquency* 30:445-473.

—— and E. Cohn (1989). "The Impact of Research on Legal Policy: The Minneapolis Domestic Violence Experiment." *Law and Society Review* 23:117-44.

—— (1991). "From Initial Deterrence to Long Term Escalation: Short-Custody Arrest for Poverty Ghetto Domestic Violence." *Criminology* 29(4):821-850.

Sieber, S. (1981). *Fatal Remedies: The Ironies of Social Intervention.* New York, NY: Plenum Press.

Skogan, W. (1990). *Disorder and Decline.* New York, NY: Macmillan.

—— and R. Block (1986). "Resistance and Nonfatal Outcomes in Stranger to Stranger Predatory Crime." *Violence and Victims* 1:241-253.

Sparks, R. (1981). "Multiple Victimization: Evidence, Theory and Future Research." *Journal of Criminal Law and Criminology* 72(2):762-778.

Sunstein, C. (1990). "Paradoxes of the Regulatory State." *University of Chicago Law Review* 57:407-441.

Veno, A. and E. Veno (1993). "Situational Prevention of Public Disorder at the Australian Motorcycle Grand Prix." In: R.V. Clarke (ed.), *Crime Prevention Studies,* Vol I. Monsey, New York, NY: Criminal Justice Press.

Viscusi, K. and R.Zeckhauser (1979). "Optimal Standards with Incomplete Enforcement." *Public Policy* 27:437-56.

Wilson, C. and N. Brewer (1992). "One and Two Person Patrols: A Review." *Journal of Criminal Justice* 20(5):443-454.

Wilson, J. and G. Kelling (1982). "Broken Windows: The Police and Neighborhood Safety." *Atlantic Monthly* (March):29-38.

Winkel, F. (1991). "Police, Victims and Crime Prevention." *British Journal of Criminology* 31(3):250-265.

Zimring, F. (1991). "Firearms, Violence and Public Policy." *Scientific American* 265(5):48-57.

—— and G. Hawkins (1973). *Deterrence: The Legal Threat in Crime Control.* Chicago, IL: University of Chicago Press.

TAKING OUT THE INTERESTING BITS? PROBLEM SOLVING AND CRIME PREVENTION

by

Adam Sutton

University of Melbourne

Abstract: National and international experience now leave no doubt that methods other than enforcement of criminal law are effective in reducing crime and associated harm. In particular, initiatives that are based on routine activity and situational theory, and those that concentrate on addressing specific, well-defined problems, have been demonstrated to have greater impact and to be less costly than "law-and-order" reactions. Despite this, problem solving and focused opportunity reduction have been comparatively neglected in Australian policy discourse. Drawing on the practical fieldwork experience of crime prevention students, this paper argues that attempts to apply opportunity reduction and problem-focused approaches often encounter obstacles and resistance not mentioned in mainstream accounts. Inclusion of these elements would ensure better understanding and appreciation of these approaches, and cement their place among strategies to challenge and displace law-and-order reactions to crime.

INTRODUCTION

National and international experience now leave no doubt that methods other than enforcement of criminal law can be effective in reducing crime and associated harm. In particular, initiatives that are based on the application of routine activity (Felson, 1987) and situational (Clarke, 1980) theory, and that concentrate on analysing and addressing specific, well-defined problems (Eck and Spelman, 1987; Hope, 1994), have been demonstrated to have greater impact and to be far less costly than

Address correspondence to: Adam Sutton, Department of Criminology, University of Melbourne, Parkville 3052, Australia.

"law-and-order" reactions. Whether the issue be crime and insecurity on housing estates (Pease, 1992; Eck and Spelman, 1987; Willemse, 1994) and transport systems (Van Andel, 1989), public disorder (Veno and Veno, 1993), drunken driving (Homel, 1988), alcohol-related violence (Homel et al., 1994; and this volume) or a wide range of other forms of law breaking, advocates of problem solving and opportunity reduction have been quietly accumulating an impressive catalogue of success stories over the last decade or so.

Despite these examples, focused problem solving has had a limited impact on Australian crime prevention policy. Several jurisdictions have embarked on well-publicised strategies in recent years. But emphasis generally has been on social programs—for example, recreational and other initiatives for young people (Dussuyer, 1991) and community development schemes aimed at strengthening informal social ties and controls at the local level (Millbank, 1992). Reservations about problem solving and opportunity reduction also have been voiced in the academic community. With some exceptions (Geason and Wilson, 1989; Homel et al., 1994; James, 1993; Veno and Veno, 1993), Australian theorists seem to have been less concerned with the achievements than with the pitfalls associated with these approaches—for example, their potential to exacerbate social divisions by privatising and commercialising security, creating housing and other fortified enclaves (see Davis, 1990), and extending less accountable forms of social control (see Shearing and Stenning, 1992). In Australian criminology, at least, these forms of prevention often are portrayed as more threatening than promising, and as more likely to complement than replace criminal justice reactions (O'Malley, 1994).

This paper explores factors that might help account for this neglect. Sympathetic to environmental approaches, it nonetheless argues that there may be more to Australian resistance than sheer bloody-mindedness. At least some of the caution is attributable to the ways in which opportunity reduction and problem solving have been conceptualised and presented. Advocates of more focused approaches tend to put emphasis on rational choice theories of offending, and to portray crime prevention as largely a matter of developing and refining appropriate techniques (Clarke, 1992). In doing so, they understate both the broader social challenges encountered once their ideas begin to be translated into practice and the potential these methods have to confront and contest, rather than simply facilitate, vested interests. More overt acknowledgment of these dimensions would help ensure that opportunity reduction and problem solving achieved proper recognition as viable tactics in the struggle to develop alternatives to law and order.

THE CONTEMPORARY CRIME PREVENTION COURSE

To illustrate and develop these arguments, this paper draws on case studies from a crime prevention course offered since 1992 by the University of Melbourne's Department of Criminology. Established and funded as part of the Victorian Government's *VicSafe* crime prevention initiatives, the full-semester (three-month) program brings undergraduate and postgraduate students together with selected participants from the Victoria Police and other government agencies. A major component, accounting for 60% of final assessment, is a team fieldwork exercise that requires students to identify and analyse specific "real-world" problems, and propose and lobby for cost-effective solutions. Issues tackled by teams in recent years include: thefts from inner-city, suburban, and remote country car parks; high rates of breaking and entering and other crime in selected suburban streets; graffiti, vandalism, and other problems at local schools; alcohol and other substance abuse at a remote Aboriginal community; bike theft and other offences on the university campus; and shoplifting at a department store and crime and insecurity in major shopping complexes.

The course gives emphasis to this "hands-on" component for several reasons. First, it is intended to assist the participants drawn from police and other government agencies to appreciate crime prevention's relevance to issues encountered during their everyday working lives, and to provide them with more suitable learning environments than passive classroom settings. Second, it gives opportunities—not often available in public policy—for people to analyse and learn from failure as well as success (Grabosky, this volume). Finally, and perhaps most importantly, practical experience can help convince participants that crime prevention requires more than a command of abstract ideas—that the most significant and in many ways most exacting challenge lies in translating theory into practice.

In undertaking fieldwork, teams are advised to employ an action research paradigm, adapted from the literature on problem-solving policing (Eck and Spelman, 1987) and situational prevention. This paradigm involves *scanning for and identifying a problem, assessing and analysing it using appropriate data, devising and costing solutions, exploring avenues for implementation,* and *sketching out an evaluation procedure* (see Figure 1). At each of these stages students can encounter hurdles rarely mentioned in textbooks: obstacles that require some reassessment of theory itself. The sections that follow provide examples under each heading.

Figure 1: Action Research Methodology (from Clarke)

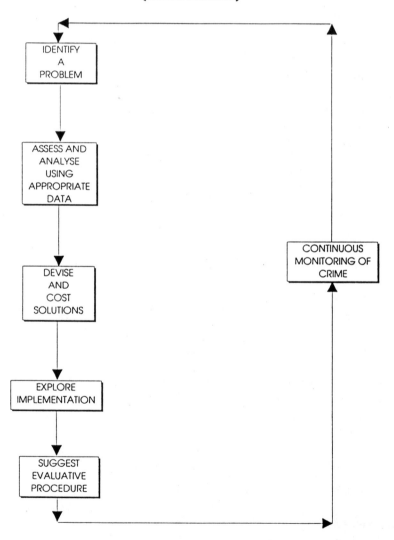

Scanning for and Identifying a Problem

In tackling the initial task of identifying and agreeing to investigate a specific problem, and persuading relevant private or public-sector organisations to give approval for a team to commence work, students could run into at least two types of difficulty. The first relates to deciding which of a myriad of problems to tackle: members confronted by this question often find themselves involved in difficult debates about their own values and priorities. The second is that even when a group agrees on an issue it can by no means assume that the organisations and agencies approached will share its concerns.

One symptom of the first difficulty is the tendency for many teams to be overambitious in initial project selection; indeed, a few have struggled to agree on any topic at all. As mentioned earlier, the course makes students themselves primarily responsible for problem identification. However, to facilitate decision making, police and other public-sector participants are singled out during the early stages and asked briefly to outline an issue that has come to their notice and that a group might address. In this spirit of "guided democracy," students are inundated during early lectures and seminars with case studies of successful prevention elsewhere in Australia and overseas, and shown selected reports from preceding years.

The vast majority of these examples emphasise specific, localised opportunity reduction and problem solving (e.g., Clarke, 1992), yet groups at this point often still find it difficult to accept that this should be their focus. Generally, the first ideas, which are submitted at the end of the fourth week, are very ambitious. Participants want to tackle such broad social issues as: relationships between police and young people; alcohol, violence, and crime; and family violence. Even when proposals do have local emphasis they tend to be comprehensive, for example, developing, costing, and advising on the implementation of crime prevention plans for a region of Melbourne, based on a thorough assessment of all of that locality's problems, services, and needs.

There is nothing intrinsically unsound in the above approach, which mirrors philosophies adopted during the 1980s in France (King, 1988) and in Great Britain (Heal, 1992). However, as most teams very rapidly acknowledge, programs of this scope can hardly be developed in a single semester. Given the intelligence, experience and commitment of the students, and their readiness—at the intellectual level, at least—to admit the need to accept some limitations, why are many so reluctant to take a more pragmatic approach?

My assessment, confirmed by feedback from some groups, is that reservations stem at least in part from a feeling that such pragmatism would be inconsistent with criminology's underlying values and philosophies. Often it seems that it is the more active and committed students— those, for example, who already had completed several years at the undergraduate level and are in, or about to commence, post-graduate studies or the final year of an honours degree—who experience the greatest difficulty in narrowing their choices.

The case that stays with me most forcefully is of a group that decided at the outset that it wanted to develop strategies to reduce criminal assaults in the home. As the team pointed out, analysis of police and other data has demonstrated unequivocally that family violence is a significant and recurring problem (National Committee on Violence, 1990; National Committee on Violence Against Women, 1992), and that there is ample scope for developing innovative programs to address it. Having made its decision, however, the group had immense difficulty in determining which line to take. One after the other, they rejected notions of early childhood initiatives, improved support for victims, and programs to try to change male perpetrators' attitudes and behaviour, on the grounds that all simply represented "band-aid" responses. One member was adamant about the need for a more comprehensive strategy that would stem from an analysis of how a basic social institution (for example, one of the major churches) was reinforcing inappropriate patriarchal values and, ultimately, abuse by males of their power.

The team eventually abandoned all its early work, and with minimal time remaining focused on situational programs to reduce theft and vandalism at a local primary school. Postmortems on the group's deliberations, however, yielded interesting insights. Basically, the students' reason for resisting unsubtle pressures ("we knew you wanted us in a car park, but we weren't going to go") was profound conviction not just about the nature and causes of offending but the role of criminologists. Without articulating it, most members had accepted that, ultimately, the origins of crime lay in deep-seated structural problems—economic and cultural dislocations, racism, gender-based power imbalances—and that the majority of "decisions" to commit offences must stem from dysfunctions in institutions such as church, school, business and politics. A criminologist's role was to challenge and try to transform such systems. All else could only be "tinkering at the edges": addressing symptoms rather than causes and displacing crime rather than generating lasting solutions.

Of course, some criminologists would dispute such assumptions. Felson (1992), for example, argues that increases in many types of crime are better understood as products of changes in "routine activities" and everyday life patterns in complex modern societies. Clarke and Weisburd (1994) contend that while displacement is always a possibility with situational prevention, research suggests it is by no means total or inevitable, and that on some occasions there may be a diffusion of benefits. However, I am convinced that in being adamant that criminology (and hence prevention) should give priority to addressing "underlying causes" this group was doing more than staking empirical claims. Instead, it was reaffirming a value position—on the need for criminologists to question and challenge power rather than comply with it—that many of us in the discipline endorse. The irony is that had they been prepared, temporarily at least, to put preconceptions aside and embark on a practical exercise, the members soon would have found more than enough challenges of this type.

This is amply demonstrated by difficulties experienced by several other teams at the problem-identification stage. I will mention just two. The first was a team wanting to apply crime prevention ideas at a major suburban shopping complex. As well as being interested in crime prevention through urban design, members had been impressed with accounts of an initiative in the Zuidplein shopping centre in the Dutch city of Rotterdam. Funded and evaluated as part of that country's five-year crime prevention pro-gram, the Zuidplein centre had been the site of extensive petty crime, and of conflicts between some young people and local traders, private security, and police. Attempts to resolve problems by intensifying security simply provided alleged troublemakers with further challenges and incentives. After forming their own committee, local businesses therefore decided on an alternative approach. Space, facilities and social support were provided for young people, who in return were asked to collaborate in the develop-ment and dissemination of a code of behaviour. Such changes seem to have helped bring about significant reductions in relevant problems (Colder, 1988).

Shopping complexes in Australia also make major demands on police services. The group, which contained several members of Victoria's police service, was keen to apply and assess similar ideas. The timing seemed good because at least one centre was about to undergo major expansion. A spokesperson contacted the owner, briefed him on the incidence of crime at this facility, and asked whether the business would cooperate in the research and development of relevant strategies. After some consideration, this overture was rejected. The businessman explained that while he was attracted to the notion of trying to "design crime prevention in" to future developments, legal advisers had advised that the risks associated with such a venture would be too great. To fund expansion, the enterprise (of which the shopping centre formed part) was being floated as a public company, with the initial share subscription target being hundreds of millions of dollars. Untimely publicity about crime problems could be damaging.

This was not the only major Victorian centre to show a marked lack of enthusiasm about the idea of having prevention groups "on site." With some exceptions, most teams wanting to base initiatives in major shopping centres experienced significant obstacles. That in Australia such centres tend to be closely owned enterprises, rather than smaller-scale collectives as is often the case in the Netherlands, helps account for at least some of these difficulties. It should be noted, though, that shopping centres were not the only entities that could stymie a project at the initial stage.

Another team, impressed by data and research on the extent of alcohol-related violence and crime (Homel and Tomsen, 1991), was keen to apply ideas for reducing the incidence of problems in and around hotels and other licensed premises. Evidence from initiatives such as Victoria's West End Forum (Victorian Community Council Against Violence, 1990) seemed to indicate that significant progress could be achieved. At the same time, Homel and his colleagues in New South Wales and in Queensland (Homel et al., 1994) had been accumulating a repertoire of methods for assisting "high-risk" locations to identify and rectify problems. The group seemed particularly fortunate in that Homel generously had agreed to make available a detailed schedule for assessing all aspects of a licensed premise's physical and social environment.

Armed with this instrument, the team set out to review a business identified as problematic through both local knowledge (e.g., regular media reports of assaults and other crime in and around the hotel) and senior Victorian police. In an effort to ensure cooperation, however, one member decided first to brief the proprietor and other relevant community interests on the group's intentions. This proved fatal. The publican made it clear from the outset that visits by the team would not be welcomed. Moreover,

despite significant evidence to the contrary, police with immediate responsibility for this region were adamant that the location did not pose any
particular concerns.

Local police also stated that they would be unable to cooperate with
fieldwork, and could not provide access to data on crime in this or other
establishments. Faced with such a boycott, the group decided that it had
no option but to assess another hotel, in another town. This time, they
were careful *not* to brief the enterprise concerned—at least not until after
on-site observations had been completed.

The experience of these two groups was perhaps at the extreme end of
the spectrum of obstacles encountered in problem selection, highlighting
an issue often glossed over in accounts of successful initiatives. Namely,
because crime prevention is about identifying difficulties and trying to
bring about change, even the most technical and apparently "neutral"
approaches can prove unsettling to established interests. To some extent,
this may also help account for difficulties encountered during the next
phase: problem analysis.

Problem Analysis and Assessment

For several reasons it was critical that the course introduce students
to problem-solving philosophies and techniques. Problem analysis can
provide a basis not just for technical success in fieldwork but for insight
into the circumstances and causes of offending and the need for flexibility
in developing responses. Too often, Australian jurisdictions have tended
to rush into solutions—whether these be Neighbourhood or other "watch"
programs, safety audits, community development, "Bonnemaison"-type
local strategies, or even group conferencing programs aimed at
"reintegratively shaming" young people—before fully appreciating the
nature of issues to be addressed. Greater emphasis on problem analysis
seemed to provide at least a possibility of overcoming this difficulty.

As Eck and Spelman (1987) have shown, problem solving can be
particularly salutary for law enforcement agencies. There is much this
sector can do in crime prevention, but program effectiveness will be
hampered if police automatically assume that they must take the dominant role (Sutton, 1994). As the Newport News (VA) and other U.S.
initiatives have shown, problem identification and problem solving can
help convince enforcement specialists that on many occasions they can
be more effective "behind the scenes": encouraging other interests such

as housing authorities, local government and resident groups to assume responsibilities.

In other words, there were good reasons for using a problem identification and analysis model as the basis for crime prevention fieldwork. It is disappointing, therefore, that this often proved the most difficult and frustrating phase. As discussed earlier, the immediate obstacle was that organisations and interests simply could deny teams access. More importantly, though, even when crime and other information was available (and it must be emphasised that, with the one exception mentioned earlier, Victoria Police at all levels have been most cooperative), it was not always useful.

This is best illustrated by the work of two teams that focused on strategies to reduce property and other "public" crimes in specific Melbourne streets. In both instances, reported crime data revealed that these locations were experiencing a comparatively high incidence of offending—mainly breaking and entering and vehicle-related problems (thefts from cars). However, while particularly useful for demonstrating that "hot spots" existed, crime data was comparatively unhelpful for illuminating what factors made these places crime prone. In particular, police systems yielded very little detail on how relevant offences were being committed and why particular targets were selected.

Of course, the most direct sources of such information are the perpetrators of such incidents, but access to them was limited. This was partly because the clear-up rate for crimes in these locations was low. However, teams often found that even when someone had been apprehended and details on modus operandi recorded, these summaries tended not to be linked to databases used for crime analysis. Several factors help explain this, not the least of them being concerns about privacy. However, as a police participant on one team later pointed out, organisational biases also affected the structuring of his department's data files. In amassing information on offenders and suspects, the focus of the police organisation is far more concentrated on its reactive role—apprehending and prosecuting particular individuals—than on broader prevention questions. Overcoming this would require not just a technical feat of linking computer files, but significant structural change within the department.

This is what Goldstein (1990) and others have been trying to achieve in their advocacy of problem-oriented approaches. What they underestimate, perhaps, is the difficulties that moves toward less-hierarchical structures and "lateral thinking" may pose for police organisations and the public. The very fact that crime prevention and problem solving have significant potential for making inroads against crime also means that they can be a major source of change and conflict. As the fieldwork group trying to assess alcohol-related violence in a small town pub found, it cannot always be assumed that police and other local organisations will welcome such disruption. As the growing literature on consultative committees and other forms of community relations (Bull and Stratta, 1994) shows, most police organisations are far more likely to opt for "managed consensus" and persuasion than head-on contests with vested interests.

It would be a mistake to dismiss this simply as bureaucratic inertia and conservatism. That in some circumstances police are authorised to resort to force—even deadly force—renders their role in modern civil society unique, and ensures that both law enforcement hierarchies and many sections of the broader public often see restricting line officers' discretion as more important than promoting it. There can be no doubt that training in and commitment to problem solving would enhance police effectiveness in crime prevention. However, bringing about these changes will require more than restructuring databases and imparting technical skills. It also demands recognition of the deep-seated social and organisational biases that can limit police involvement in proactive roles—particularly ones with the potential to stimulate conflict with influential groups (see Moore, 1992). Without such reassessment, police will continue to "ignore the obvious" and react to crime rather than try to address its underlying causes.

Devising and Costing Solutions, and Avenues for Implementation

This became apparent for teams that worked their way through to the phase of devising and costing solutions, and onto identifying problems and attempting to get them implemented. Here, too, there were challenges rarely mentioned in textbooks or case study collections. For many groups, the greatest obstacles lay not so much in technical problem solving as in the social task of persuading relevant interests to assume responsibility for solutions.

Again, a good example emerged from the work of the teams addressing public or semi-public crimes in selected suburban streets. As mentioned, police databases did not always lend themselves to problem analysis.

However, one pattern of offending was so distinctive as to make solutions appear relatively straightforward. At least eight cases of vehicle breaking-and-entering during an eight-month period analysed by one team were against cars parked in a single location: an open parking area located underneath a small block of home units. The units were on a corner block close to an intersection, and at night the parking area itself was poorly illuminated. Capacity for surveillance directly underneath the building, which was raised on concrete pillars, was poor. The property lacked fences, gates, or other barriers to segregate private from public, and offenders wanting to break into or damage cars needed only to take two or three steps from the public footpath before being able to commence work.

This was a classic example of poor design and lack of defensible space (Newman, 1972), where a range of possible prevention measures was immediately apparent. Proposals itemised and costed by the team included: better lighting (perhaps movement-activated) for the car park area, a fence and lockable gates to screen off cars and separate the home units' grounds from the public footpath and street, mirrors to improve surveillance, and warning signs to deter unauthorised visitors.

The problem then became one of identifying and persuading relevant parties to authorise and pay for this work. From interviews with residents in the building where cars were being damaged, the prevention team had ascertained that most were renting and had been there a short time. While discussions confirmed that they were the principal victims, it hardly seemed reasonable to expect them to foot the bill for security. As one tenant pointed out, one likely reward for improving the property in this way would be a rent increase, which she personally would have difficulty in meeting. A more logical candidate to meet the expenses was the building's owner. This person, however, proved difficult to locate.

Eventually, the team decided that the best it could do in the short term was prepare a leaflet for residents, notifying them of the problem and suggesting they try to exert pressure on the landlord to implement some or all of the team's recommendations. In the longer term, the group recommended two amendments to Victoria's Residential Tenancies Act. The first would enable tenants experiencing high rates of breaking and entering, vandalism or other property-related victimisation to appeal to the Residential Tenancies Tribunal for an order compelling the landlord to implement appropriate measures. The second would authorise prospective tenants to require individuals or businesses offering a property for lease to produce a list of relevant offences on, or in the vicinity of, these premises.

Before implementing these proposals there would need to be a close assessment of ethical, economic and other social implications. Reviewing them, though, I find it remarkable that such controversial ideas should have been generated as a consequence of the application of techniques that many in the field almost automatically brand as traditional and conservative. However, such controversies may be far more common than is generally acknowledged. Most student fieldwork groups reaching the implementation-and-evaluation phase found themselves puzzled about, and wanting to argue with, business and other interests who seemed reluctant even to consider proposals. Even in the more general literature on situational prevention and problem solving, where conflict aspects tend to be played down, it is not unusual to find references to the need for vested interests to act more responsibly. Work by Homel and colleagues (1994) on crime in and around licensed premises in Queensland's Gold Coast, and by the Victorian Community Council Against Violence (1990) in Melbourne's King Street are good examples. So, too, is Field's (1993) recent work on motor vehicle theft. While crime reduction may be a factor for business, it often is subordinated to other goals, such as profit and market share. As Challinger (1991) points out in his analysis of Telecom Australia's program to reduce theft from and vandalism to public phones, even this exemplary model of prevention within the business sector was not driven by a desire to reduce offending per se. Instead, the perceived need to maintain the volume of calls sold from these outlets was the issue that finally drove Telecom to refocus administrative responsibilities, and to introduce a range of target hardening and other situational measures.

DISCUSSION

In presenting accounts from fieldwork experience, emphasis has been on obstacles encountered rather than successes achieved. In fairness to the individuals and teams concerned, it should be emphasised that most did not allow difficulties to deter them from devising and developing cost-effective, practical and sometimes quite novel proposals. Despite the limited time available, moreover, quite a few teams made significant progress toward persuading public- and private-sector organisations not just that problems existed but that prevention was worth taking seriously.

A review and assessment of reports in the last three years reveals an impressive picture of what "ordinary" cross-sections of people can do, once given respite from routine environments and encouraged to be innovative and to think laterally.

However, there is value sometimes in refraining from celebrating advances and focusing instead on the issues that can make it difficult for people or programs to move forward. As mentioned at the outset of this paper, despite their demonstrated successes, opportunity reduction and other "problem-focused" approaches are still far from entrenched as key components in Australian crime prevention policy. Reviewing setbacks and frustrations experienced by some teams has helped draw attention to system biases that militate against more widespread adoption of these approaches. Accounts of such resistance also are useful for reminding academic critics that problem solving and opportunity reduction often involve far more than the application of technical skills. In addition to having practical potential for reducing offending, used in the right ways focused crime prevention can be a powerful mechanism for helping expose inequities and contest the status quo. In developing and documenting these approaches, it is important that attention be given not just to technical aspects but to these dimensions. No discussion of crime prevention can be complete unless it takes account of the contexts in which techniques are applied, the interests "owning" (see Veno and Veno, 1993) and affected by these measures, and the resistance encountered.

Too often these dimensions are missing. Indeed, a review of the ways opportunity reduction and other focused forms of crime prevention have been presented brings to mind a story about the English novelist Evelyn Waugh. A long-term acquaintance of some fame, possibly Randolph Churchill, recently had been operated on for a tumour, that proved non-cancerous. Most people sent expressions of relief and support. The novelist's only comment was that it was typical of British medicine to rush someone to hospital, open him up and remove the only part of him that was not malignant.

It would hardly be fair to argue that, in failing to mention the contests and controversies that often accompany opportunity reduction and problem-based approaches to crime prevention, criminology has been exhibiting similar perversity. Nonetheless, the fact that both advocates and critics often gloss over these elements does say something about the discipline. As much as any social science, criminology has been afflicted by the twin curses of what Mills (1970) terms "abstracted empiricism" and "grand theory." In crime prevention, as in other fields, criminologists too frequently have allowed themselves to become engrossed either in applying techniques in ignorance of broader social contexts, or in postponing any action in favour of locating the emergence of specific crime prevention practices in the context of broader interpretative schemes. As characterised by Mills and, more recently, the Foucauldians and left realists, I see these dichotomies between action and theory as spurious. Experience with the crime prevention course alone makes clear that exposure to practice can sometimes stimulate much sharper understandings of subtle and dispersed economies of power (Foucault, 1977; Lukes, 1974, see also Kritzman, 1988) than might be possible from purely theoretical expositions. My sense is that exposure to fieldwork often can also leave students more able and inclined to fight for change—albeit limited—than any number of hours in seminar rooms.

The purpose of this paper has been to defend opportunity reduction and other problem-focused approaches as critical components in any crime prevention strategy. In taking this stance, however, I have argued that expositions must include, rather than exclude, the more contentious elements. I should emphasise, moreover, that unlike some advocates I do not see pragmatism as comprising the totality of crime prevention. The ultimate rationale for becoming engaged in this sphere of policy is to help find ways to displace law and order, not just with practices that are more effective but with alternative frameworks for understanding and dealing with offending and insecurity. Given the scope of this challenge, crime prevention cannot simply consist of interventions that "work" in a limited technical sense. Disciplines such as medicine have long been aware that prevention must encompass both specific programs (for example, diet, exercise, and lifestyle regimes) and broader activity (such as campaigning to improve sanitation and other services for disadvantaged communities, and opposing the aggressive marketing strategies of cigarette companies). Crime prevention also must acknowledge the need to be effective in politics and advocacy as well as in specific practical contexts. Even for these more general roles, however, opportunity reduction and other focused approaches have value. As this paper has shown, they can provide rich opportunities for unmasking and coming to grips with sources of power that, while often dispersed and unobtrusive, nonetheless often play critical roles in frustrating constructive reform and keeping law and order intact as the only viable political response to crime. Criminologists who have genuine interest in challenging this hegemony should never underestimate the value of focused action.

Acknowledgements: The author thanks the Government of Victoria's *VicSafe* crime prevention program for its continuing support for the Contemporary Crime Prevention course. This paper reflects and has emerged from an ongoing and energetic dialogue with students, whose course contributions, critical comments, and other feedback are gratefully acknowledged. Thanks also to Steve James and Rob White for comments on an earlier draft.

REFERENCES

Bull, D. and E. Stratta (1994). "Police Community Consultation: An Examination of its Practice in Selected Constabularies in England and New South Wales, Australia." *Australian and New Zealand Journal of Criminology* 28(3):237-249.

Challinger, D. (1991). "Less Telephone Vandalism: How Did It Happen?" *Security Journal* 3(2):111-119.

Clarke, R. (1980). "Situational Crime Prevention: Theory and Practice." *British Journal of Criminology* 20:136-147.

—— (ed.) (1992). *Situational Crime Prevention: Successful Case Studies.* Albany, NY: Harrow and Heston.

—— and D. Weisburd (1994). "Diffusion of Crime Control Benefits: Observations on the Reverse of Displacement." *Crime Prevention Studies* 2:165-183.

Colder, J.C. (1988). *Het Winkelcentraproject: Preventie van Kleine Criminaliteit.* The Hague, NETH: Staatsuitgeverij.

Davis, M. (1990). *City of Quartz.* London, UK: Verso.

Dussuyer, I. (1991). "The Good Neighbourhood Program." Paper presented at the Seventh Annual Conference of the Australian and New Zealand Society of Criminology, Melbourne, October.

Eck, J. and W. Spelman. (1987). *Problem-Solving: Problem Oriented Policing in Newport News.* Washington, DC: Police Executive Research Forum.

Felson, M. (1987). "Routine Activities and Crime Prevention in the Developing Metropolis." *Criminology* 25(4):911-931.

—— (1992). "Routine Activities and Crime Prevention: Armchair Concepts and Practical Action." *Studies on Crime and Crime Prevention* 1:30-34.

Field, S. (1993). "Crime Prevention and the Costs of Auto Theft: An Economic Analysis." *Crime Prevention Studies* 1:69-92.

Foucault, M. (1977). *Discipline and Punish.* London, UK: Peregrine Books.

Geason, S. and P. Wilson. (1989). *Crime Prevention: Theory and Practice.* Canberra, AUS: Australian Institute of Criminology.

Goldstein, H. (1990). *Problem-Oriented Policing.* New York, NY: McGraw-Hill.

Heal, K. (1992). "Changing Perspectives on Crime Prevention: The Role of Information and Structure." In: D. Evans, N. Fyfe and D. Herbert (eds.), *Crime, Policing and Place: Essays in Environmental Criminology.* London, UK: Routledge.

Homel, R. (1988). *Policing and Punishing the Drinking Driver: A Study of General and Specific Deterrence.* New York, NY: Springer-Verlag.

—— M. Hauritz, R. Wortley, J. Clark and R. Carvolth (1994). *The Impact of the Surfers Paradise Safety Action Project.* Brisbane, AUS: Griffith University Centre for Crime Policy and Public Safety.

—— and S. Tomsen (1991). "Pubs and Violence: Violence, Public Drinking, and Public Policy." *Current Affairs Bulletin* 68(7):20-27.

Hope, T.J. (1994). "Problem-Oriented Policing and Drug-Market Locations: Three Case Studies." *Crime Prevention Studies* 2:5-31.

James, S. (1993). "Public Housing Security and Tenant Empowerment: Lessons from an Australian Experience." Paper presented at the Fifth International Research Conference on Housing, Montreal, Canada, (July).

King, M. (1988). *How to Make Social Crime Prevention Work: The French Experience.* London, UK: National Association for the Care and Resettlement of Offenders.

Kritzman, L.D. (1988). "Foucault and the Politics of Experience." In: L.D. Kritzman (ed.), *Michel Foucault: Politics, Philosophy, Culture (Interviews and Other Writings 1977-1984).* New York, NY: Routledge.

Lukes, S. (1974). *Power, A Radical View.* London, UK: Macmillan.

Millbank, S. (1992). "Crime Prevention: A South Australian Perspective." In S. McKillop and S. Vernon (eds.), *National Overview on Crime Prevention.* Canberra, AUS: Australian Institute of Criminology.

Mills, C.W. (1970). *The Sociological Imagination.* London, UK: Penguin.

Moore, M.H. (1992). "Problem-Solving and Community Policing." In: M. Tonry and N. Morris (eds.), *Crime and Justice: A Review of Research,* vol 15. Chicago, IL: University of Chicago Press.

National Committee on Violence (1990). *Violence: Directions for Australia.* Canberra, AUS: Australian Institute of Criminology.

National Committee on Violence Against Women (1992). *National Strategy on Violence Against Women.* Canberra, AUS: Australian Government Publishing Service.

Newman, O. (1972). *Defensible Space. People and Design in the Violent City.* London, UK: Architectural Press.

O'Malley, P. (1994). "Neo-Liberal Crime Control: Political Agendas and the Future of Crime Prevention in Australia." In: D. Chappell and P. Wilson (eds.), *The Australian Criminal Justice System: The Mid 1990s*. Sydney, AUS: Butterworths.

Pease, K. (1992). "Preventing Burglary on a British Housing Estate." In: R. Clarke (ed.), *Situational Crime Prevention: Successful Case Studies*. Albany, NY: Harrow and Heston.

Shearing, C. and P. Stenning (1992). "From Panopticon to Disney World: the Development of Discipline." In: R. Clarke (ed.), *Situational Crime Prevention: Successful Case Studies*. Albany, NY: Harrow and Heston.

Sutton, A.C. (1994). "Community Crime Prevention: A National Perspective." In: D. Chappell and P. Wilson (eds.), *The Australian Criminal Justice System: The Mid 1990s*. Sydney, AUS: Butterworths.

Van Andel, H. (1989). "Crime Prevention that Works: the Care of Public Transport in The Netherlands." *British Journal of Criminology* 29:47-56.

Veno, A. and E. Veno. (1993). "Situational Prevention of Public Disorder." *Crime Prevention Studies* 1:157-175.

Victorian Community Council Against Violence (1990). *Violence In and Around Licensed Premises*. Melbourne, AUS: Department of Justice.

Willemse, H.M. (1994). "Developments in Dutch Crime Prevention." *Crime Prevention Studies* 2:33-48.

THE "DREAM" OF MULTI-AGENCY CRIME PREVENTION: PITFALLS IN POLICY AND PRACTICE

by

Reece Walters

Victoria University of Wellington

Abstract: During the 1980s, terms such as interagency or multi-agency cooperation, collaboration, coordination, and interaction have became permanent features of both crime prevention rhetoric and government crime policy. The concept of having the government, local authorities, and the community working in partnership has characterized both left and right politics for over a decade. The U.S. National Advisory Commission on Criminal Justice Standards and Goals in the U.S., Circulars 8/84 and 44/90 released by the U.K. Home Office, and the British Morgan Report—coupled with the launch of government strategies in France, the Netherlands, England and Wales, Australia, and, more recently, in Belgium, New Zealand, and Canada—have all emphasized the importance of agencies working together to prevent or reduce crime. This paper draws upon recent Australian research and critically analyzes multi-agency crime prevention. It suggests that agency conflicts and power struggles may be exacerbated by neo-liberal economic theory, by the politics of crime prevention management, and by policies that aim to combine situational and social prevention endeavors. Furthermore, it concludes that indigenous peoples are excluded by crime prevention strategies that fail to define and interpret crime and its prevention in culturally appropriate ways.

INTRODUCTION

The partnership approach in crime prevention has for some time been seen as an essential ingredient in government crime policy (U.S. National

Address correspondence to: Reece Walters, Institute of Criminology, Victoria University of Wellington, P.O. Box 600, Wellington, New Zealand.

Advisory Commission on Criminal Justice Standards and Goals, 1975; Sampson et al., 1988; Morgan, 1991), and continues to receive support in Europe, England and Wales, Australia, New Zealand, and Canada (see van Dijk, 1995; Crawford and Jones, 1995; Presdee and Walters, in press). Central to notions of partnership is the networking of agency expertise, collaborating ideas, and involving the community in decision making and management. However, this concept of government and community agencies combining resources for crime prevention purposes has reported with mixed results. Earlier studies by Baldwin and Kinsey (1982) identified the theoretical and ideological contradictions of interagency goals, and Bradley et al. (1986) questioned the extent to which equal power could be achieved while the police remained the major stakeholders in crime-related efforts.

Other concerns have been raised by Blagg et al. (1988) and Sampson et al. (1988), who assert that there are fundamental fractures in multi-agency initiatives and that there are practical limitations that are expressed through tensions and power struggles over control, ownership, resources and management. Other works suggest that multi-agency approaches are best utilized for situational crime prevention methods. When problem-oriented methodologies are applied to opportunity-reduction strategies, agency-specific involvement is focused. However, when social and situational methods are combined, the key players are diverse and their role is undetermined—with confusion, power plays and inaction at their peak (Gilling, 1994).

Issues of structure, leadership, consultation, ownership, training, resources, and publicity have been examined by Liddle and Gelsthorpe (1994b), who conclude that such factors mitigate both success and failure. The extent to which a multi-agency crime prevention approach will achieve its objectives may be contingent upon sound planning and management, and also upon a range of political uncertainties within local agencies and local communities, where personal and organizational agendas inhibit active coordination (Liddle and Gelsthorpe, 1994b). Community empowerment and ownership are notions frequently applied by policymakers and practitioners wanting to implement multi-agency crime prevention programs; yet, recent work by Duke et al. (1996) reports that communities and agencies may refuse to take ownership of an issue, preferring to deflect responsibility to those primarily responsible.

At its core, multi-agency crime prevention is a mix of agency ideology, expectations, expertise, resources and commitment that together produce an array of informal and formal networks, resulting in both meaningful and problematic outcomes (Liddle and Gelsthorpe, 1994a). This paper will critically analyze multi-agency crime prevention endeavors by drawing upon recent findings from an Australian evaluation. In doing so, it will examine how some of the barriers to multi-agency cooperation discussed above can be tackled in light of government commitments to the new managerialism, to theoretically flawed notions of crime prevention, and to culturally exclusive processes of planning and development.

LESSONS FROM AN AUSTRALIAN CRIME PREVENTION STRATEGY

Planning and Development

In August 1989, the South Australian Government (one of Australia's six state governments) launched a five-year statewide crime prevention strategy with ten million dollars (Australian) in funding. Although other Australian states had embarked upon various crime prevention endeavors, this clearly marked the most significant attempt in that country's history to address crime prevention through means other than traditional criminal justice approaches (Presdee and Walters, in press). Fueled, in part, by initiatives in England and Wales, France, and the Netherlands— and responding to political and electoral pressure to combine "law and order" policies with something new—this state released a project called "Together Against Crime." This project involved a mix of both social and situational approaches, with a commitment to involve people from senior officials (such as cabinet ministers) to local residents. A review of the South Australian crime prevention strategy was undertaken by LaTrobe University in Melbourne. The research began in August 1993; a final report was submitted in July 1994.

This crime strategy began with a select group of five officials touring the U.S., Canada, and Europe during January and February 1989 in search of "principles of best practice" for use at home (Presdee and Walters, 1994:15). One member of this "study tour," who would eventually head up the strategy, commented that the tour findings raised three significant problems for an Australian-based policy: (1) the transportation of practices adopted in Europe (particularly those involving interagency interaction);

(2) the need for cultural inclusion; and (3) the difficulties involved in effectively evaluating a diverse mixture of social and situational programs (such as surveillance cameras, curfews, changes in environmental design, as well as education, employment, and self-esteem courses for youth and a variety of others) (Sutton, 1991). These criticisms were to prove prophetic.

The findings of the study tour were tabled in the South Australian Parliament in mid-1989 and in August of the same year. Two policy documents entitled "Confronting Crime—South Australia's Crime Prevention Strategy" and "Together Against Crime, a Policy Plan for South Australia" were officially launched by the Attorney-General. In essence, these documents expressed the need to integrate existing criminal justice practices with community-based initiatives. This partnership approach was advertised using the slogan "Together We Can Arrest Crime" and presented to an electorate as a constructive endeavor aiming to curb rising crime rates.

In December 1989, the Labour Government was returned to office. It announced that, during the first financial year, 1.3 million dollars (Australian) would be allocated to six projects: home security and safety for the elderly; recreational activities for street kids; computer mapping of crime data to identify high-risk areas; "School Watch" to secure school buildings; extension of the Blue Light program (teenage discos supervised by police officers); and the Police Deputies Club, a program promoting crime prevention in primary schools (South Australian Government, 1990).

The first 18 months of the strategy proved a difficult period for the Crime Prevention Policy Unit (later named the Crime Prevention Unit (CPU)) to implement policy. A major contributing factor was the way in which the cabinet conflated the role of the CPU and the implementation of policy (Presdee and Walters, 1994). In late 1988, the South Australian Cabinet envisaged the administration of the crime prevention strategy to be undertaken by a "secretariat" within the Attorney-General's Department. Following the launch of the strategy, a subsequent cabinet document, dated October 1989, referred to the secretariat's role in the following way: "The Crime Prevention Committee be serviced by an executive comprised of representatives of the Attorney-General's Department, the Police Department and other relevant agencies" (Cabinet Document AGD 114/89 quoted in Presdee and Walters, 1994:26).

The original function of the CPU was to administer the strategy. However, at the time of the policy's launch, the CPU was viewed as comprising representatives from police and other departments and directed to service a crime prevention advisory group (Presdee and Walters, 1994). It is clear that little thought was given to precisely how the strategy would be implemented and managed. This lack of direction produced an organizational vacuum that took time to fill. At the time of the policy's launch, the structure was not in place to administer the funding of the projects mentioned above. Setting up the bureaucratic structure created delays in implementation during which several community agencies, acting upon the good faith of the government, began to question the extent to which this new government crime policy was anything more than a broken electoral promise (Presdee and Walters, 1994). There were no empirically based reasons why the aforementioned projects were targeted for funding.

The introduction of a community-based program that made no mention of how state networks of power could ever connect with local networks of power was profoundly flawed from the outset. As one member of the CPU commented, almost 18 months into the strategy there was "still no clear means of getting $10 million to the community" (Presdee and Walters, 1994:27). Another member reported how the original policy's lack of focus created problems for implementation: "We were labouring with these original objectives and the Unit dropped them and realised very early on in the piece that they were not reflecting what we were about...we had no coherent aims and objectives in a global sense for the Strategy" (Presdee and Walters, 1994:28). The member also noted that "[b]y the end of 1990 the Crime Prevention Unit and the Crime Prevention Strategy was in a state of paralysis" (Presdee and Walters, 1994:49).

In July 1991, members of the CPU set about drafting a new mission statement and attempting to create a strategy that, in their minds, had not been made clear. Following a series of planning seminars, and after 18 months of the policy's designated five years, the CPU articulated a strategy made up of four major components:

(1) Coalition Against Crime;
(2) Local Crime Prevention Committee Program;
(3) Aboriginal Program; and
(4) Exemplary Projects.

The Local Crime Prevention Committee Program involved local agency workers and residents coming together and devising strategies for local problems. The Aboriginal Program specifically targeted the needs of the Nunga and Pitjatjatjarra communities, and the Exemplary Projects were nine discrete programs targeting issues of high priority or public concern— for example, family violence, drinking in and around licensed premises, youth, crime and the elderly, and so on (Presdee and Walters, in press). The latter three components of the overall strategy endorsed and encouraged interagency interaction; yet, the cornerstone in matters of multi-agency collaboration was the Coalition Against Crime, whose membership was drawn from police, local government, justice, Aboriginal Affairs, youth, education, social welfare, health, private sector, and a number of voluntary agencies. Its function is explored in more detail below.

Multi-agency Crime Prevention at the State Level

During 1986 in England and Wales, Margaret Thatcher chaired a ministerial group on crime prevention (U.K. Ministerial Group on Crime Prevention, 1989). In contrast, South Australia's Coalition Against Crime involved more than government ministers. It attempted to harness key agency personnel as well, with the express purpose of addressing crime collaboratively. In a structural sense, this was the most powerful group ever to come together in South Australia's history to be advisers to the Cabinet (Presdee and Walters, 1994). The group comprised government and shadow ministers for the police, justice, and Attorney-General's departments; chief executive officers of departments (such as Health, Social Welfare, Community Services, Aboriginal Affairs, Corrections, Education, Police, Central City Mission, Attorney-General's, and Youth); senior members of the business community; district court judges; and a number of senior policy managers from a range of public sectors. Yet, from its outset, it was never made clear by either the Crime Prevention Unit or the politicians involved exactly what these 50 powerful officials were meant to be doing. Initial Cabinet papers reveal that this group was to act as both a community receptor and an instigator of interagency involvement. It was also seen as having a management function over departmental expenditures. However, the group's earliest meetings (two in the first 12 months) were characterized by argument, indecision, absenteeism and a failure to agree upon a fundamental purpose. In an attempt to provide the group with a focus, the CPU convened a workshop that became known as the "red dot day." The manager of the CPU described this event as follows:

> So they went through this amazing, interesting process, including the Premier [head of government] removing himself from the chair and letting the facilitator take over and really direct what they were on about[,] which was going through a brainstorming exercise[,] throwing around a whole lot of different ideas and then reflecting on some of those ideas and doing their red dot voting. You know the red dot exercise? Everyone gets five red dots. After you've done your brainstorming and identifying of various priorities you then have the discretion to put your five dots against five issues. So they all got their five red dots and had great fun working around this big room with all the butcher's paper [quoted in Presdee and Walters, 1994:58].

The Labour Government in South Australian had already launched a crime prevention policy prior to the state's election; yet, here it was, almost two years later, trying to understand that same policy using butcher's paper and professional facilitators.

Once the politicians and the state's senior executives and businesspeople had allocated all their dots, a count was taken. "Corrections" was identified as the most important issue in crime prevention, followed by community education involving community pride and youth, morality, multi-cultural issues, and parenting. For the first time in the strategy's 18-month life, the Coalition Against Crime, which was to be the peak adviser to the overall crime policy, was provided with a sense of direction.

Prior to this, it had proven difficult to arrange and coordinate meetings and venues, unable to agree upon which programs should be funded, and unable to generate any workable output from this powerful body that was to steer the strategy and exert influence on relevant agencies. In spite of providing focus, the red-dot exercise was unable to provide the group with cohesion. Working parties (on urban and housing design; alcohol, drugs and crime; violence prevention; and community-based crime prevention) were established but were poorly facilitated and lacked structured follow-up. Moreover, ideological differences and competing interests prohibited any effective collaboration. The police, for example, strongly favored programs that aimed to restore discipline, respect for authority and a sense of community morality. Social workers argued for increases in welfare. Educators pushed for early intervention programs and changes to state schooling curriculums. Businesspeople supported employment programs, church groups supported values and family, Aboriginal Affairs supported cultural awareness, and so on. These interpretations were to create a melting pot of ideologies that had an impact on the way in which policies unfolded.

Crime prevention initiatives are often embarked upon without coherent theory or practical expression. As mentioned above, problem-oriented methodologies, more suited to situational measures, are frequently applied to social crime prevention strategies—with unsuccessful or uncertain outcomes (Gilling, 1994). This breach between policy and practice is partly explained by the under-theorized nature of the crime prevention discourse (Sutton, 1994). Emerging from this are a number of spin-off terms that have compromised the objectives of preventing crime. Terms such as "crime reduction," "community safety," "community well-being," and "communities in partnership" have all become key features of this expanding discourse we call crime prevention (Ekblom, 1994). In sum, these terms have been loosely applied to a mixture of social and situational strategies without regard for practical expression, producing a vast number of disparate programs and unsophisticated evaluations (Ekblom and Pease, 1995).

Crime prevention (as it was in South Australia) cannot be seen as an organic process. It must be theoretically sound, focused and consistent. The South Australian Government attempted to integrate various agencies into a policy that was unclear in the minds of the public servants managing the strategy, who were content with a fluid and non-proscriptive policy that they felt would promote diversity and community participation. Yet, it is clear that this organic approach eventually isolated agencies and community personnel, including large numbers of Aboriginal people. Furthermore, it became apparent that Coalition members were not only presenting their given philosophy of crime and its prevention, but were clearly attempting to use the forum for the personal advantage of their given agency or organization. In other words, the Coalition Against Crime simply became another opportunity to gain access to funding—an attitude that would promote tension and competition and pronounce the death of any workable and focused activity.

The articulation of key areas almost two years into the strategy's life (an activity that was seen to provide the group with momentum and purpose) came at a point when the Crime Prevention Unit, which was responsible for the management of the strategy, had all but given up on the Coalition, referring to it as "schizophrenic" and lacking "cohesion."

Commenting on the red dot day, a senior CPU policy officer said, "...I think it was just seen as priorities for the Coalition, maybe the Minister saw it differently, but I don't think the Unit picked it up as priorities for the strategy." The group was seen as having conflicting agendas, bargaining for funds, and generally attending for political reasons. The CPU manager summed up this powerful interagency crime prevention group as follows:

> [they were] six monthly interval meetings, a real hotch-potch of agenda items, politics mixed into the whole melting pot and you've got a group of individuals who come along every six months because the Premier or Attorney-General was there and they thought it might be important to sit there representing"my sector" [Presdee and Walters, 1994:60].

The public servants managing the crime strategy were faced with a dilemma: how could they make use of this high-profile group that was seen as the pinnacle of the strategy? The PU manager commented: "We recognised that with the political overtones we were getting we couldn't just pronounce the Coalition's death. We had to find some way to make something of it. We came up with the Core group. It was generally agreed that this was the best way to go."

The CPU embarked upon a downgrading of the Coalition and produced a slimmed-down version, cutting its membership from 50 to 10—an action that could not resolve the various tensions inherent in the group. One of the remaining Coalition members, who became a Core Group member, succinctly described how the groups functioned:

> One of the original objectives was the Coalition members would come together, develop ideas and do something as a group, but also importantly take those ideas back into their own institutions, organisations and agencies and I don't think that has happened. It was just a question of coming together at a meeting, saying a few clever things and then going home again... [Presdee and Walters, 1994:175].

This "influential" interagency grouping did not see the end of the strategy's initial five-year period; it was seen as a liability and eventually (unofficially) disbanded.

Regardless of the power or status of a given group, clear direction and purpose is crucial to any long-term and workable outcome. Specific tasks must be addressed by agencies with the appropriate expertise and resources. It is of little value to have irrelevant players, regardless of their prestige or influence, involved in matters that are not necessarily their concern. It is at this point that politics intervenes in a most dangerous way. When agencies are invited largely for political reasons, they eventually withdraw interest—but not before creating friction and conflict with other organizations with which they are supposed to be building important bridges. Inclusion is important but, as Gilling (1994) and Liddle and Gelsthorpe (1994a) have suggested, their inclusion must be relevant and focused. Providing a powerful body like the Coalition Against Crime with a mixture of social and situational crime prevention objectives—from increasing lighting and security outside hotels to developing environmentally safe architecture to an array of youth and family programs—created more agency barriers than it broke down, resulting in both inaction and the group's eventual demise. With the collapse of this group, it is interesting to examine how local and community agencies handled similar briefs, and the effect of the breakdown on local crime prevention initiatives.

Multi-agency Crime Prevention at the Local or Community Level

With the state's senior executives and politicians failing to provide a network of expertise that would see practical expression through crime prevention programming, the Crime Prevention Unit clung to the community as the linchpin of the state's crime strategy. Modeled on the Bonnemaison scheme in France, the Local Crime Prevention Committee Program aimed to gain access to existing local structures, and to generate interest and support for innovative crime prevention issues. Communities (defined by local council boundaries) throughout the state were invited to submit proposals to the CPU for funding. Advertisements were placed in local newspapers calling upon interested community people to attend a series of public meetings to address crime in their areas. From these meetings, local working groups or committees (with between 12 and 20 representatives from predominantly government-funded agencies) were formed and prepared proposals for Attorney-General Department's funding. These proposals (some up to 60 pages long) included community demographics, crime profiles, and a range of community-based initiatives intended to prevent or reduce particular areas of community concern.

Defining "communities" within council jurisdictions proved exclusionary and off-putting for a wide range of agencies and community personnel.

As one community project officer (responsible for coordinating a local crime prevention strategy) said,

> ... council simply can't be a key player, but must be an equal player. I mean the rules and regulations imposed on our committee run counter to a community development model. I know people who won't get involved because it's seen as a council program... Councils are very parochial and often don't work together and because local committees work around council boundaries there's often this ridiculous view that you can't do anything outside your boundary.

Eventually, 22 of 27 areas were successful in receiving government support, each one providing a collection of both social and situational initiatives aimed at preventing a range of criminal activities. In all, over 500 programs were either spawned or supported, with youth and family violence targeted most frequently. Within the same local committee, some members called for increased police, more neighborhood-watch-type activities, and changing the physical environment to reduce opportunities for offending, while others emphasized employment and recreational programs for young people.

Any positive outcomes, whether intended or not, were more likely to reflect the efforts of individual people who made programs work rather than the combined input of relevant agencies. Similar to other components of this crime prevention strategy, management was to have an impact on the way this policy was implemented. Indecision over program structure, funding formulas, criteria for selection, staffing, training, and resources hampered the involvement of local communities, who sought direction and leadership from the Crime Prevention Unit.

Local committees had formed across the state, involving a range of agencies and residents seeking to develop and implement local strategies for local needs. Integral to local development was the notion of multi-agency collaboration. Indeed, it was eventually specified in the CPU's funding guidelines as a prerequisite for initial funding allocations. Thus, funding guidelines stipulated the need to demonstrate in local strategy plans "improved co-ordination between services" and it was made clear that "...allocations are intended to ensure flexibility of local agencies to stimulate change and co- operation." The local committees were formed, but as one chairperson described the process, it did not end there. Without a clear mandate on exactly what they were expected to do, any notion of a multi-agency approach was thwarted:

> ... I mean we just didn't know what was going on. We got a group of interested people together and said now what! I rang the Unit on several occasions and they couldn't tell me anything and I was the chairperson who couldn't tell the committee anything. It was really confusing and it wasn't until some time in 1992 (12 months on) that we knew what we were about and what we were supposed to do [Presdee and Walters, 1994:69].

The lack of government guidelines created overwhelming expectations at the local level. Communities developed unrealistic approaches in a blind attempt to secure funding. This quest to secure grants left local communities grappling with strategy plans that were clearly beyond their reach. Community representatives continually sought advice and direction about local activities. They saw the value in linking agency resources, yet they lacked expertise in mobilizing the existing resources in their communities. The CPU failed to provide this direction because it wanted to empower communities and allow them to "go their own way" and not appear to be interfering. As one CPU project officer put it, "Some (community) project officers wanted a road map, but the Unit couldn't provide the answers because the Unit was going along the path as well, but that wasn't a bad thing because the strategy wasn't meant to be proscriptive"

Clearly this was a bad thing. Indeed, it was to prove one of the most significant factors in the lack of agency involvement. Agency personnel continued to withdraw support or interest as they witnessed a program lacking cohesion and structure. As one of the community project officers commented:

> The CPU ran the professional line until they finally came clean about the Strategy, that is, the CPU finally admitted their lack of knowledge and this was a first for them. They should have been up front from the outset rather than leaving communities on their own without support [Presdee and Walters, 1994:32].

Fundamental questions—such as, what is multi-agency crime prevention? how should it function? what is it expected to do? who is expected to contribute?—were stumbled upon in practice rather than defined in the early stages of policy development. If multi-agency crime prevention processes are to contain concepts that foster positive action, then some basic problems need to be resolved. Crawford and Jones (1995) identified the need for greater conceptual differentiation when discussing the partnership approach, one which defines what is expected of agencies by way of both input and output.

Multi-agency collaboration and multi-agency networking, for example, are two different concepts that are often conflated. Networking is a process of interaction where agencies discuss and exchange ideas and information and, wherever possible, provide assistance and advice. Collaboration is much more than mere interaction, and involves the active input of interagency resources to bring about both community or institutional change (Presdee and Walters, 1994). The networking of agencies at all levels is clearly important for meaningful collaboration. Identifying the landscape of expertise, developing referral systems, pooling ideas and exchanging information are useful for consolidating a network of knowledge, services and programs. The process of interaction provides a plank for collaborative output based on issues of collective concern. Collaborating and networking will naturally intersect, operate at formal and informal levels, and produce worthwhile outcomes. Yet, importantly, there is a distinction that often explains the level to which an agency is *capable* of contributing and not necessarily what they are *willing* to contribute: the extent to which a smaller agency can collaborate may be limited by that agency's resources, personnel, and expertise. These agencies may experience a "structural subordination" (Clarke and Mayhew, 1980), placing them in a less influential and powerful position than other agencies.

In such cases, the input of the smaller agency must be contextualized in terms of its capacity to contribute. Too often smaller agencies extend their commitment beyond their means in order to gain equal status with larger agencies. The larger government-funded organizations (particularly the crime-related ones of police, corrections, and justice) tend to dominate. They become the power brokers as their resources and their frontline dealings with crime place them in an elevated position of authority. Yet the work of smaller government and voluntary agencies is crucial. Many of these agencies provide the history and life of a given community. They are, in a sense, better placed to mobilize existing structures and resources. Yet the conflict between and within agencies remains a formidable barrier to coordinated approaches. Sampson et al. (1988:482) concluded:

> ... one of our most consistent findings is the tendency for interagency conflicts and tensions to appear, in spite of co-operative efforts, reflect-

ing the oppositions between state agencies at a deep structural level.
We have also found consistent and persistent struggles over limited
resources, power and prestige.

Competing interests and structural tensions over power, prestige and
ownership are pitfalls likely in any area involving multi-agency activity. Yet,
when they exist within an unspecified framework of crime prevention and
multi-agency crime prevention, the term "multi-agency" further loses
meaning and direction for practical expression.

The lack of direction, community feedback and consistent management
by the South Australian Crime Prevention Unit was most detrimental when
viewed in light of Aboriginal involvement. During the planning of the
strategy, the Attorney-General (the politician leading the policy) argued
that "Aboriginal culture is the keystone of this program, not a white
bureaucracy." What that government failed to grapple with was that, for
Aboriginal people, crime prevention carried different meanings from those
projected by white populations. Structural alienation remains the single
most important issue to Aboriginal peoples, while racism and social and
economic dislocation are central to understanding Aboriginal offending.
As one senior Aboriginal public servant reported:

> ... Aboriginal people have been going along to local crime prevention
> committees where they feel the white committee members are the
> source of crime... But what happens is what I call an "add on bureau-
> cracy" where people like to create another bureaucracy to deal with the
> obvious and what happens is that the bureaucracy begins to compete
> for its own market share... There are a whole lot of other social
> development issues which we find it difficult to get resources for and
> here's this big bucket of money for crime prevention [Presdee and
> Walters, 1994:158-159].

Crime prevention for Aboriginal communities is often expressed in
terms of addressing racism, poverty, unemployment, police brutality,
sickness, education, and family support. Multi-agency crime prevention
initiatives that assert mono-cultural understandings of crime and its
prevention often exclude minority groups. When crime prevention is
determined by white bureaucracies, and, in turn, is targeted at minority
groups that are seen as the problem, involving Aboriginal agencies in some
collaborative effort will probably only achieve their superficial input. From
the 22 local committees, eight were strategically developed in districts with

high populations of Aboriginal people. Over 150 representatives sat on committees in these areas, yet only 14% were Aboriginal. Many attended simply to avoid being seen as not interested, not wanting to cut off future funding sources. However, their input was seen as largely tokenistic from within their own communities and, generally, worthless. Unless Aboriginal Australians feel a sense of ownership and inclusion, positive outcomes for Aboriginal people will remain few in number.

In one instance, an Aboriginal community in the state's far west (Yalata) had used crime prevention funds to build a basketball court to alleviate youths' boredom and promote recreation. Within the same community, a white magistrate flew to Yalata from the capital (1,200 miles) every month and set up a courthouse in a vacant tin shed. In spite of temperatures soaring to 120 degrees, over 150 cases were heard by this one magistrate in less than a day. All cases were heard in English, even though English is largely not spoken in this remote Aboriginal community. As a result, most defendants were sentenced with little knowledge of what they had done, what was said in court, or what was going to happen to them. Defendants were sentenced to jail, dragged out by police officers, and placed in vans awaiting transportation across the desert to the nearest prison. Such an example of criminal justice in Australia is the exception, not the rule; yet, in early 1994, it was common practice in this isolated Aboriginal town. Interestingly, when Aboriginal people were asked why they had not used crime prevention funding to appoint a court interpreter or to increase legal aid (choosing instead to build a basketball court), the response was simple: "At least the kids can play basketball, but that over there, it'll never change, can't do nothing about that."

Multi-agency crime prevention faces dilemmas at deep structural and cultural levels that extend beyond agency conflicts and power, and that involve long histories of dislocation and neglect. For years Aboriginal communities were not consulted over government policies that resulted in massive changes to Aboriginal lifestyles and development. In more recent years, it has become politically astute, and, in some instances, legally required, to consult Aboriginal people over matters involving land and public policy. Yet Aboriginal people are acutely aware of history and often remain skeptical over government policies that promise higher standards of living, education, welfare and so on. When their inclusion is without adequate consultation and ownership, Aboriginal people experience a naive form of racism operating within government, where white bureaucracies are seen to be determining their needs and best interests.

When multi-agency approaches fail to consider adequately cultural differences in interpretation, planning, and implementation, they often exclude those groups most in need of assistance.

The Australian research echoes many of the research findings from elsewhere that were discussed in the introduction. The experience in South Australia clearly highlights the risk that multi-agency approaches in crime prevention (particularly those that proliferate every conceivable approach to preventing crime) may produce more problematic outcomes— e.g., inter-agency conflicts, cultural alienation, and community resentment—than beneficial ones.

GENERAL DISCUSSION

The bulk of multi-agency crime prevention efforts to date have emerged from policies that lack any consistent theory. Consequently, multi-agency crime prevention has been widely defined and applied with various interpretations. It continues to receive government support. This cross-fertilizing of expertise and resources while embracing community needs has been both politically popular and economically viable. Yet this devolution of state responsibility for rising crime rates to communities within a framework of partnership has occurred with little regard for pragmatic outcomes.

Much of the earlier theoretical contribution to crime prevention (specifically situational crime prevention) came from Clarke (1980), Clarke and Mayhew (1980), and Clarke and Cornish (1985), with the development of opportunity theory—in particular, the rational choice perspective. This body of work created clear connections between theory and the development of situational prevention techniques. More recent work by Clarke and Homel (in press) extends Clarke's earlier rational choice scheme (Clarke, 1992), providing a framework that places greater emphasis on the psychological and social contexts of offending. Clarke and Homel (in press) integrate concepts of shame (Braithwaite, 1989), moral commitment (Grasmick and Bursik, 1990), neutralization of guilt (Sykes and Matza, 1957), and peer pressure (Sutherland and Cressey, 1966) in their typology. In light of the dearth of criminological theorizing about the mixture of social and situational prevention activities, and the continued efforts by governments to combine the two, Clarke and Homel's work is a welcome development.

It is also important that multi-agency practices be understood as operating within broader political trends seeking efficiency and cost-effectiveness. Government policies driven by neo-liberal economic theory have produced a new ethos in both the public and private sectors (O'Malley, 1994). Emerging from this movement is a new order of management—involving purchase agreements, output statements, performance indicators, strategic plans, and so on—all part of this new era of efficiency and productivity (Pollitt, 1993).

This new managerialism, driven by ideologies of economism and strategic rationalism, has created a restructuring of the public sector across Western society. The merging of public and private enterprises for economic prosperity and capitalist development has rapidly become a discourse of government policy and practice (McLaughlin and Murji, 1995). In keeping with this neo-liberal economic approach, public sectors in Australia and, particularly, New Zealand, are expected to demonstrate how their departments have fulfilled their contractual agreements with government. In other words, have they provided all the services government contracted with them to provide?—that is, has their "core business" been satisfactorily delivered?

These new political directions are touching all levels of business and management, both public and private (Kelsey, 1995). This creates a conundrum and something of a challenge for those organizations charged with responsibility for coordinating a multi-agency crime prevention strategy. Crime prevention units must sell the multi-agency approach to organizations where crime is not part of their core business. Health authorities, for example, often engage in work that intersects with crime (e.g., drugs, alcohol); yet, government resources are not allocated for crime prevention purposes. Crime prevention is not part of their "purchase agreement." There is little inducement for such agencies to become involved and, if they do participate, it is likely to be as minimally as possible. Crime prevention units end up acting like brokers, attempting to convince agencies that crime prevention is worthwhile for their organization. In New Zealand, crime prevention has, in some instances, been written into departmental contracts as either a core business or a strategic result area. For example, Social Welfare, Education, Te Puni Kokori Maori Affairs, Justice, and other departments are required to demonstrate involvement in national crime prevention endeavors. Yet, it is not clear what this actually means, and, moreover, there is considerable disparity in the extent to which government departments become involved.

Throughout the Australian research many organizations expressed nervousness about linking resources with other agencies that they perceived as potential threats to their business. For example,

> ... There's this thing called "client poaching"... If you've got your little patch of clients you don't give them up for anybody, because they're worth stats to you. And also, regardless of whether you're [sic] offering is of great value to the client—they won't let you have them... [Presdee and Walters, 1994:165].

Multi-agency collaboration becomes a fashionable, lip-service term receiving no meaningful commitment. Organizations will publicize their networking efforts for political advantage, but they will not share their clientele or resources with other agencies that they see as their competitors. While governments continue to interpret merging and restructuring as economically viable and efficient, multi-agency crime prevention remains a limited concept threatened by agency tension and competition for resources. The new managerialism may, therefore, provide underpinnings that conflict with notions of partnership and collaboration, creating interagency tensions.

CONCLUDING DISCUSSION

Multi-agency crime prevention is a complex and problematic concept. As a crime policy it should be considered with caution. It is a broadly interpreted concept frequently operating within shifting discourses of crime prevention. Moreover, at its core, there exist agency power struggles, ideological tensions, competing interests, and cultural disparities—all forming a melting pot of diverse expectations, processes, and outcomes. Further compounding the problem are the political climates in which multi-agency prevention continues to be favored. In countries like Australia and New Zealand, it remains a popularized and fashionable concept, promoting notions of government and community working together. However, these political movements may have economic rationalist and new managerialist structures demanding cost-effectiveness and accountability that run counter to models demanding a collective enterprise. By design, they assert individualism and impose distinct boundaries via contractual arrangements with agencies whose services are purchased by government.

The extension of those services into other worthwhile areas is constrained by purchase agreements requiring the delivery of itemized products.

The purpose, expectations and desired outcomes of interagency approaches must be clearly articulated. Both formal and informal networks are capable of producing worthwhile outcomes; yet, it is important to define the nature of the interaction as well as the intervention and the desired outcome. The findings of the Australian research confirm those of earlier works in suggesting that multi-agency crime prevention should be focused, thus allowing the importation of relevant experts to unite information and resources. Eclectic crime prevention programming creates dangers at a practical level. It is here that social crime prevention strategies are vulnerable. Without defined tasks and desired outcomes the known pitfalls of agency power struggles over leadership and ownership are exacerbated, resulting in damaging and potentially long-lasting schisms between the agency and the community. Theoretically consistent proposals are more likely to produce beneficial effects. Situational crime prevention measures are equally vulnerable to agency power plays and the vagaries of broader political trends; yet, their clearly defined objectives and methods provide them with a structure to take advantage of selected multi-agency expertise.

Advocates of social crime prevention policies who wish to use multi-agency approaches must specify the aims and processes of intervention in ways that control the shortcomings mentioned above. Once multi-agency crime prevention models are put in place, they must be carefully managed. The Australian research painfully demonstrates how potentially worthwhile interagency programs simply fall apart without well-planned, well-managed, and culturally-inclusive administration. It is here that those charged with the responsibility for overseeing multi-agency crime prevention must ensure that policies have distinct mechanisms capable of producing specific results.

Without grounded theory and clearly identifiable targets of intervention capable of producing measurable outcomes, however, multi-agency crime prevention loses its ability to be effectively operationalized. This should be the goal of policy officers in the business of crime prevention, so that interagency crime prevention enterprises are not seen, as the following fieldworker describes, as just a dream: "... we all know about the dream of inter-agency collaboration, lots of promises but no-one ever carries anything through..." (Presdee and Walters, 1994:175).

Acknowledgements: I wish to acknowledge Mike Presdee, University of Sunderland, England, for his helpful ideas and feedback on this paper.

REFERENCES

Baldwin, R. and R. Kinsey (1982). *Police, Power and Politics.* London, UK: Quartet.

Blagg, H., G. Pearson, A. Sampson, D. Smith and P. Stubbs (1988). "Inter-Agency Co-ordination: Rhetoric and Reality." In: T. Hope and M. Shaw (eds.), *Communities and Crime Reduction.* London, UK: Her Majesty's Stationery Office.

Bottoms, A. (1990). "Crime Prevention in the 1990's." *Policing and Society* 1:3-22.

Bradley, D., N. Walker and R. Wilkie (1986). *Managing the Police.* Brighton, UK: Wheatsheaf.

Braithwaite, J. (1989). *Crime, Shame and Reintegration.* Cambridge, UK: Cambridge University Press.

Bright, J. (1993). "Crime Prevention: The British Experience." In: K. Stenson and D. Cowell, *The Politics of Crime Control.* London, UK: Sage.

Clarke, R.V. (1980). "Situational Crime Prevention: Theory and Practice." *British Journal of Criminology* 20:136-147.

—— (ed.) (1992). *Situational Crime Prevention: Successful Case Studies.* Albany, NY: Harrow and Heston.

—— and P.M. Mayhew (eds.) (1980). *Designing Out Crime.* London, UK: Her Majesty's Stationery Office.

—— and D. Cornish (1985). "Modeling Offenders' Decisions: A Framework for Policy and Research." In: M. Tonry and N. Morris (eds.), *Crime and Justice: An Annual Review of Research,* Vol. 6. Chicago, IL: University of Chicago Press.

—— and R. Homel (in press). "A Revised Classification Of Situational Crime Prevention Techniques." In: S. Lab (ed.), *Crime Prevention at a Cross-roads.* Cincinnati, OH: Anderson.

Crawford, A. and M. Jones (1995). "Inter-Agency Co-operation and Community-Based Crime Prevention: Some Reflections on the Work of Pearson and Colleagues." *British Journal of Criminology* 35(1):17- 33.

Crawford, A. (1996). *The Local Governance of Crime. Appeals to Community and Partnerships.* Oxford, UK: Clarendon Press.

Duke, K., S. MacGregor and L. Smith (1996). *Activating Local Networks: A Comparison of Two Community Development Approaches to Drug Prevention.* Paper 10. London, UK: U.K. Home Office Drugs Prevention Initiative.

Ekblom, P. (1994). "Towards a Discipline of Crime Prevention: A Systematic Approach to its Nature, Range and Concepts." Paper presented at the 22nd Cropwood Conference, Preventing Crime and Disorder (London, UK).

—— and K. Pease (1995). "Evaluating Crime Prevention." In: M. Tonry and D.P. Farrington (eds.), *Building a Safer Society: Strategic Approaches to Crime Prevention.* (Crime and Justice: A Review of Research, Vol. 19.) Chicago, IL: University of Chicago Press.

Gilling, D. (1994). "Multi-Agency Crime Prevention in Britain: The Problem of Combining Situational and Social Strategies." In: R.V. Clarke (ed.), *Crime Prevention Studies,* Vol. 3. Monsey, NY: Criminal Justice Press.

Grasmick, H. and R. Bursik (1990). "Conscience, Significant Others, and Rational Choice." *Law and Society Review* 34:837-861.

Kelsey, J. (1995). *The New Zealand Experiment: A World Model for Structural Adjustment?* Auckland, NZ: Auckland University Press.

Liddle, A.M. and L. Gelsthorpe (1994a). *Crime Prevention and Inter- Agency Co-operation.* Crime Prevention Unit Series Paper 53. London, UK: Home Office Police Department, Police Research Group.

—— (1994b). *Inter-Agency Crime Prevention: Organising Local Delivery.* Crime Prevention Unit Series, Paper No. 52. London, UK: U.K. Home Office Police Department, Police Research Group.

McLaughlin, E. and K. Murji (1995). "The End of Public Policing? Police Reform and 'the New Managerialism.'" In: L. Noaks, M. Levi and M. Maguire (eds.), *Contemporary Issues in Criminology.* Cardiff, UK: University of Wales Press.

Morgan, R. (1991). *Safer Communities: The Local Delivery of Crime Prevention Through the Partnership Approach, Report of the Standing Conference on Crime Prevention.* London, UK: Her Majesty's Stationery Office.

O'Malley, P. (1994). "Neo-Liberal Crime Control: Political Agencies and the Future of Crime Prevention in Australia." In: D. Chappell and P. Wilson (eds.), *Crime and Justice in Australia—The Mid 1990's.* Sydney, AUS: Butterworths.

Pollitt, C. (1993). *Managerialism and the Public Services.* Oxford, UK: Blackwell.

Presdee, M. and R. Walters (1994). *Policies and Practices of Preventing Crime: A Review of South Australian Crime Prevention Strategy.* Melbourne, AUS: National Centre For Socio-Legal Studies.

—— (in press). "Policies, Politics, Practices: Crime Prevention in South Australia." In: P. O'Malley and A. Sutton (eds.), *Crime Prevention in Australia—Current Issues and Contemporary Problems.* Melbourne, AUS: Federation Press.

Sampson, A., H. Blagg, P. Stubbs and G. Pearson (1988). "Crime, Localities and the Multi-Agency Approach." *British Journal of Criminology* 28:478-493.

South Australian Government (1990). Confronting Crime. Adelaide, AUS: Attorney-General's Department.

Sutherland, E. and D. Cressey (1966). *Principles of Criminology* (7th ed.) New York, NY: J.B. Lippincott.

Sutton, A. (1991). "The Bonnemaison Model: Theory and Application." In: B. Halstead (ed.), *Youth Crime Prevention—Proceedings of a Policy Forum Held 28 and 29 August 1990*. Canberra, AUS: Australian Institute of Criminology.

—— (1994). "Crime Prevention: Promise or Treat?" *Australian and New Zealand Journal of Criminology* 27(4):5-20.

Sykes, G. and D. Matza (1957). "Techniques of Neutralization: A Theory of Delinquency." American Sociological Review 22:664-670.

U.K. Home Office (1991). *Safer Communities: The Local Delivery of Crime Prevention through the Partnership Approach.* London, UK: U.K. Home Office.

U.K. Ministerial Group on Crime Prevention (1989). *Progress Report.* June 1989. London, UK: British Parliament.

U.S. National Advisory Commission On Criminal Justice Standards And Goals (1975). *A National Strategy to Reduce Crime. A Report by the National Advisory Commission on Criminal Justice Standards and Goals.* New York, NY: Avon Books.

van Dijk, J. (1995). "In Search of Synergy: Coalition Building Against Crime in the Netherlands." *Security Journal* 6:7-11.

SITUATING CRIME PREVENTION: MODELS, METHODS AND POLITICAL PERSPECTIVES

by

Robert White

University of Melbourne

Abstract: This paper provides a commentary on the politics surrounding different crime prevention models and methods. It argues that conflating particular models with particular methods can unnecessarily undermine the acceptance of certain approaches as being appropriate "crime prevention" interventions. The paper presents three abstract models of crime prevention—conservative, liberal and radical—and discusses how diverse methods can be separated from these models, and need to be examined, understood, and used in broader political context.

The aim of this paper is to explore different models of crime prevention as a means to highlight important theoretical and political issues that too often remain submerged in "practical" discussions of the merits or otherwise of particular strategies and techniques. It will be demonstrated that "crime prevention" in general is not a uniform or homogeneous area of conceptual development and policy orientation. Rather, ingrained in the very process of designing crime prevention strategies are certain core assumptions and political choices. Acknowledgement of these is essential if we are to make sense of existing and potential conflicts within the field, and evaluate the impact of particular approaches as adopted by criminal justice authorities.

Address correspondence to: Robert White, Criminology Department, University of Melbourne, Parkville, Victoria 3052, Australia.

MODELS OF CRIME PREVENTION

Crime prevention is contentious. Different people have different conceptions as to what it ought to refer, and different agendas in terms of the kinds of organisational and philosophical objectives they are trying to meet. To appreciate the nature of these differences it is useful to consider three abstract models of crime prevention (see Figure 1). Each model identifies the key focus and concepts of a particular approach, preferred strategies of intervention, dominant conception of "crime," the role of the "community" as part of the crime prevention effort, and relationship to "law-and-order" strategies. In devising these models I have drawn upon the work of Iadicola (1986), McNamara (1992), and Cunneen and White (1995), and have concentrated mainly on those community-based strategies that attempt to stop offending behaviour before it occurs.

The models presented below are "ideal types" in the sense of being one-sided and exaggerated examples of broad outlooks on crime prevention (see Freund, 1969). They are, nevertheless, based upon actual cases and real programs. As is always the case with ideal types, however, the substantive work of specific writers or the insights provided in particular approaches (e.g., crime prevention through environmental design, situational prevention) do not necessarily conform in their entirety to one or another of the abstract models. In practice, few researchers and criminal justice officials restrict their attention to just one particular model or perspective, but instead draw upon a wide range of ideas and practices associated with the different models. The models are useful in that they do reflect broad tendencies at the practical and policy level, and they alert us to significant strengths and weaknesses in existing strategies.

In addition to allowing us to distill certain key elements of crime prevention that are evident in existing field-based approaches, the models also highlight the *political differences* within criminology and the criminal justice system. As such, the models are sometimes drawn upon, implicitly or explicitly, as a rationale for accepting or rejecting particular methods or techniques associated with crime prevention. In other words, the models themselves (regardless of theoretical efficacy or explanatory power) can be used *ideologically* to create boundaries between and around particular intervention techniques and philosophical legitimacies. A conservative thus may reject certain methods because of their presumed association with liberal or radical styles of crime prevention. Conversely, a radical may reject other techniques simply on the grounds that they appear to form an essential part of the conservative approach.

These are important issues, for it could well be argued that this *conflation of theoretical model with practical method* is potentially damaging in a number of ways. First, from an analytical perspective, it means that the contextual nature of community crime prevention gets lost in terms of specific ideological content or political connotation. We are presented with a scenario that says this model and this technique are necessarily conservative, liberal or radical—regardless of human intent, local conditions, history of an area or population group, or general political-economic circumstances.

Second, such a conflation can have particular consequences in relation to the politics of crime prevention generally. For example, such rigid and sharp distinctions between perspectives (and related methods of primary choice) can provide easy ground for the general retreat from discussions of ideology and values by those who see themselves first and foremost as "neutral," "scientific" and "professional" in their crime prevention endeavours. Indeed, there appears to be a tendency in much conventional crime prevention discourse to, in effect, exclude discussion or acknowledgement of the politics of crime prevention altogether (e.g., see Clarke, 1992; and, for further comment, Sutton, this volume).

On the other hand, where ideological and political difference is more overtly addressed, there may be an inclination to create a dichotomy between approaches—such as crime prevention versus social development. While the differences here are explicitly recognised and dealt with, the end result may substantially be the same as those cases where the political implications of one's crime prevention approach are not formally acknowledged. Thus, theoretical demarcations of this nature can cloud over the issue of choice of methods. This occurs when particular methods are associated in simplistic and narrow fashion with specific political stances, and excluded on the basis of their tie to a particular ideological framework (e.g., see Coventry et al., 1992).

The politics of crime prevention is of crucial concern in terms of the means and goals that we adopt in making the world a safer and better place. Accordingly, how we construe crime prevention politics has significant ramifications for how we ultimately intervene at a practical level. But for the moment, let us turn to a brief examination of three crime prevention models. The models have been devised to reflect the major political divisions within criminological theory generally (see White and Haines,

1996), and are based upon previous reviews of concrete programs, practices and strategies in the crime prevention field (see Iadicola, 1986; McNamara, 1992; Cunneen and White, 1995).

Figure 1: Models of Crime Prevention

Conservative Model of Crime Prevention	
Key Concept	crime control
Main Strategy	opportunity reduction
Main Crime Focus	conventional "street" crime
Concept of Criminality	rational choice
Crime Response	protection, surveillance
Role of Community	auxilliary to police
Limitations	based on social exclusion, narrow definition of crime

Liberal Model of Crime Prevention	
Key Concept	social problem
Main Strategy	opportunity enhancement
Main Crime Focus	conventional "street" crime
Concept of Criminality	individual or social pathology
Crime Response	correct deficits, improve opportunities
Role of Community	self-help, community development
Limitations	based on limited resources, narrow definition of crime

Radical Model of Crime Prevention	
Key Concept	social justice
Main Strategy	political struggle
Main Crime Focus	crimes of the powerful, conventional "street crime"
Concept of Criminality	marginalisation, social alienation, market competition
Crime Response	social empowerment, reduce inequality
Role of Community	social change agents
Limitations	based on shared consciousness/solidarity, wide definition of crime

Conservative

The traditional or conservative model of crime prevention starts from the premise that the basic issue is one of *crime control*. It is founded upon the notion that the key issue is adherence to the law, and that law enforcement and crime prevention should therefore be directed at addressing potential and current violations of the law. Crime is ultimately seen as a matter of incentives and deterrents. Basically, this model combines elements of classical criminological theory (with an emphasis on voluntarism and personal responsibility) with rational choice theory (which sees human behaviour primarily in terms of calculated perceptions of the costs and benefits of particular courses of action). The solution to crime is to increase the costs and *reduce the opportunities* for the commission of crime, and to increase the likelihood of detection.

In order to reduce opportunity, this perspective is usually linked to measures that are designed, first, to increase *surveillance* in the public domain (e.g., on the street, in the workplace, on public transport) through police patrols, citizen watch committees, closed-circuit cameras and confidential hotlines; and, second, to build better *protection* into existing and new buildings, major complexes and residential areas through innovative design techniques, target hardening, and private security agencies.

The model generally does not rest upon a sophisticated notion regarding the causes of crime (particularly with respect to specific patterns of criminality associated with particular social groups). Rather, it abstractly assumes that crime is a matter of choice and opportunity, and therefore open for anyone to pursue given the right circumstances. Most of the model's practical application is in the areas of *conventional crime* or "street crime," and workplace crime involving low-level theft, pilfering and passing on of confidential information. Issues relating to corporate crime would revolve around the actions of particular individuals, not the overall context and activities of business generally.

Traditional crime control measures rely upon members of the community playing an *auxiliary role* in support of official law enforcement agencies. The "community" ought to be part of the eyes and ears of the police, and merely assist their crime control efforts. Citizen participation is channelled through official committees (such as police-community consultative committees, neighbourhood watch committees, etc.) that are, and under this model ought to be, predominantly police-led and that reflect a crime control agenda.

The limitations of this model are, first, the narrow definition of crime and criminality that ignores the material differences in a situation that may influence individual and group behaviour; and, second, its reinforcement of a general climate of fear of crime and suspicion of others, thus fragmenting communities. In particular, such an approach tends to be based upon *social exclusion* insofar as it privileges those who have the means to buy protection and surveillance, and to target those who do not.

Politically, such a model tends to be complementary to the "law-and-order" enforcement agenda, with an emphasis on maintenance of public order and protection of private property, and a perception that criminality is at least in part due to lack of individual self-control and lack of respect for authority. The "broken windows" argument proposed by Wilson and Kelling (1982) in the U.S., which deals with issues of suppressing symptoms of disorder and cycles of urban decline, provides an example of an approach that is redolent with the ideas of the conservative model of crime prevention. This type of approach can readily justify selective attention on certain types of behaviour and activity, and on particular population groups. The emphasis is on control and exclusion.

Liberal

The mainstream, or liberal, approach to crime prevention views crime as a *social problem* linked to particular individual deficits and group disadvantages. It is based upon the idea that people, rather than crime control, should be the starting point for change, and that reform is needed at the level of individual and collective circumstance. In essence, this perspective views the issue as one of *opportunity enhancement* for those people who have been in some way divorced from adequate or appropriate work and school opportunities.

The main focus in this perspective is on "at-risk" individuals and groups who exhibit some sign of propensity to engage in conventional crime. After identifying those people who have or are most likely to engage in this sort of crime, the strategy is to intervene to correct the *pathology* at the heart of the problem. This may be directed at fixing personal defects (e.g., dealing with drug addiction) and/or attempting to introduce programs that tap into problems affecting a whole community of people (e.g., an intensive literacy program for non-English-speaking migrants).

This model borrows from theories such as biological and psychological explanations (generally oriented toward attributes of the individual), strain theory (with an emphasis on the disjuncture between cultural goals and structural means to attain these), labelling theory (where positive self-esteem is linked to personal resources and the nature of state intervention in one's life), and some (later) forms of left realism (which emphasise multi-agency approaches at a local level). The difference between the criminal and the non-criminal is one dictated by biological, psychological and social circumstance.

Improving opportunity for individuals and groups means early intervention and concerted efforts to get communities to use their own resources to improve social and economic conditions. The "community" is seen as a resource in its own right, and the idea is to *mobilise community members* in a range of self-help measures such as volunteer sports programs, social groups, camps, leisure activities and so on. This may require the assistance of professional community workers, specially trained police officers and social workers, and financial aid in the form of short-term government grants for training or recreation projects. As such, the approach endorses a *community development* perspective with respect to the issue of crime prevention—one which rests upon multi-agency cooperation and the sharing of ideas and resources.

The limitations of this model are, first, that it tends to deal only with conventional crime, and, second, that it does not question the reasons why there is inequality to begin with, and why some people are especially disadvantaged under the present social system. More fundamentally, this approach tends to be restricted solely to *local initiatives,* and thus is severely limited in accessing the material resources necessary to transform the life chances and opportunities of people and communities.

Politically, the model tends to run counter to or to challenge many aspects of the law-and-order response to crime and crime control. It is proactive in nature, and operationally oriented toward *problem-solving* rather than dealing with the specific instances of crime per se. The work of Coventry et al. (1992) in Australia, which deals with issues of youth crime prevention, constitutes an approach that basically encapsulates many of the ideas of the liberal model. Here the emphasis is on providing "developmental" types of program for young people, and openly acknowledging the problems of "disadvantage" in designing any type of state or non-government intervention in the lives of the young. The approach is oriented toward institutional reform and better resource allocation.

Radical

The radical, or conflict, model of crime prevention sees law and order as an arena of *political struggle*. Crime and criminality is historically and socially constructed, and is best understood as reflecting structural social divisions and inequalities. It is most closely associated with Marxist criminological theory (which sees class analysis as central to an understanding of crime under capitalism), feminist criminological theory (with gender relations and power differentials the major focus), and critical criminology (referring here to perspectives that examine the oppression and marginalisation of groups on the basis of class, gender, ethnicity, sexuality, and race). The key concept is that of fundamental social change, which should be directed at enhancing the material well-being, social rights and decision-making power of the majority in society.

The biggest crime is seen to be that of economic *inequality* and social and economic *marginalisation*. These are seen to affect specific categories of women, ethnic minority groups and the working class in particularly negative and entrenched ways, and to fundamentally shape the social patterns of criminality, the interventions of the criminal justice system, and the processes associated with victimisation. Both conventional crime and crimes of the powerful are seen to stem from entrenched power relations favouring those who own and control the means of production and thus the overall allocation of community resources. Rather than focusing on aspects of crime control, or individual or group adjustment to existing structural conditions, this model favours an approach that challenges the basis of marginalisation, social alienation and market-driven competition.

The goal is one of *social justice*, the linchpin to addressing many of the problems associated with street crime, corporate crime and crimes of the state. Social justice in this context refers to achieving structural changes in the organisation of basic social institutions and in the allocation of community resources. Rather than studying social problems in terms of their impact on specific individuals (e.g., the "poor" as a focus for research or programme development), this model examines the relationship between groups (e.g., the rich and the poor) and attempts to address the structural imbalances and inequalities that give rise to the problem (e.g., of poverty) in the first place.

The main strategies favoured by this model therefore include action to *reduce inequality* through such measures as redistribution of community resources and reallocation of wealth (e.g., via taxation and nationalisation), and to encourage *social empowerment* by democratising all facets of community life (e.g., in the workplace, at the local neighbourhood level, in the household), including areas such as policing and crime prevention. Addressing the specific problem of crime means actively intervening on wider issues of political and economic importance, as well as organising community members to exercise control over their safety and well-being at the local level. This includes action being taken on issues such as pollution; inadequate public transport, housing, or educational facilities; sexual harassment; racist violence; and problems related to conventional crime and antisocial behaviour. Community members are seen as crucial agents of social change in their own right.

The limitations of this model are, first, that there invariably is resistance to any strategy that challenges the status quo (including that exerted by state officials such as the police), and, second, communities are often fractured ideologically into many different groups that do not share the same beliefs and attitudes about social justice or the same perceptions regarding appropriate crime prevention strategies. *Shared consciousness and group solidarity* do not preexist; they must be forged in struggle and are part of a difficult and long-term political process.

Politically, the model is in opposition to the law-and-order approach. It sees the logic of crime control as one essentially directed at containing the effects of economic crisis and differences in social power, rather than dealing with the generative causes of crime under capitalism. Furthermore, any enhancement of the power of the state (via, for example, greater police powers) is seen as problematic insofar as the state itself is implicated in the maintenance of the status quo. Nevertheless, the precise role of the state is, arguably, seen to be open to contestation and change.

An example of work that reflects many of the ideas contained in the radical model is that of Sim et al. (1987) in Britain, which summaries the practical interventions of critical criminologists in areas such as prison abolition, police issues, racism, women's struggles and the struggles in Northern Ireland. Crime prevention in this instance refers to confronting and dealing with the crimes of the powerful (e.g., abusive and skewed use of state power, the actions of the capitalist class, white racism) through a

variety of action campaigns. Key issues in this instance are conscious-
ness-raising, collective mobilisation and critique of the status quo.

THEORY, POLITICS AND PRACTICES

The foregoing models present in abstract form three broad perspectives
on crime prevention. We can distinguish these specific theoretical models
from particular crime prevention techniques and practices, which may or
may not pertain to each model. To put it simply, while a wide range of
specific crime prevention methods can be identified (see, for example,
Clarke, 1992), these methods are not in and of themselves necessarily
linked to any of the particular models presented above. This has a number
of implications, particularly with respect to how we think about crime
prevention both generally and with regard to the importance of the context
within which particular methods are actually adopted.

Rather than simply responding to crime after the fact, recent attention
to crime prevention has focused on specific ways in which to modify the
physical and social environment. Changes to the *physical environment*
have included such measures as:
- better streetscape and building design;
- improved lighting in public spaces;
- use of close-circuit TVs, remote sensors, and electronic keycards;
- installation of deadlocks and alarms;
- design and location of parking areas;
- rapid cleaning of graffiti;
- property marking and identification; and
- traffic calming and creation of green belts.

Attempts have also been made to extend the range of *surveillance* of
local neighbourhood activities, involving such measures as:
- establishment of Neighbourhood Watch committees;
- reintroduction of police beat patrols in inner-city areas;
- encouragement of "natural surveillance" through residential planning;
- employment of private security guards in residences and businesses;
- use of "information officers" on buses and trains;

- monitoring of factory/business pollution by environmental action groups;
- anti-racist/anti-fascist organisations; and
- community watch committees to prevent police harassment.

In addition, attempts have been directed at enhancing *citizen participation* programs that are not crime-centered per se. These would include, for example:

- sports and recreation programs;
- community clean-up campaigns designed to make a local environment more attractive and conducive to positive social life;
- provision of alcohol and substance abuse health and counselling services;
- needle exchange programs and AIDS counseling;
- employment of youth and community workers to provide a range of health, welfare, and leisure services;
- local employment initiatives, usually funded by short-term government grants; and
- campaigns against poverty and unemployment.

The present concern is not with whether such techniques and practices are "successful," although to evaluate this we would need to know more about the specific implementation and outcomes of particular tactics, campaigns and programs in selected locales. Instead, the crucial point to be made about crime prevention is that it is not, nor has it ever been, politically neutral. That is, the wide variety of techniques, practices and policies encompassed under the broad crime prevention umbrella have differential social impacts. How certain measures affect different groups of people depends very much on how they are implemented and on the political basis for their particular implementation.

For example, as discussed in depth elsewhere (see White and Sutton, 1995) the development of some types of "situational prevention" responses overwhelmingly reflects the social interests and financial capacities of the economically well-off in the community. Located within a generally conservative model of crime prevention, the adoption of some types of protective and surveillance measures serves to reinforce the crime control agenda of the right-wing law-and-order lobby, and to orient programs and policing strategies toward containment objectives rather than dealing with the wider conditions that generate crime. Particular kinds of crimes are targeted over others (e.g., commercial property theft), and the intention is to create a hostile environment for certain categories of people (e.g., unemployed young people who do not have the financial capacity to purchase goods and services). Economic and social exclusivity is built into such crime prevention strategies.

On the other hand, liberal or radical models of crime prevention may draw upon similar types of techniques and practices, but the objectives and context greatly alter the meaning and consequences for the people involved (for a similar discussion, see Sutton, this volume). An organised street presence, for example, may be essential to ensure freedom from sexual harassment, racist attacks or police violence. In this process the use of video cameras, recording devices, street lighting, self-defence training and community action groups may bear a structural similarity to traditional law enforcement and crime prevention strategies, although the *social content of the practices* is of course very different. Here the concern is with the social empowerment of more powerless and vulnerable groups, and their active engagement in controlling their social landscapes directly.

Generally speaking, however, environment modification techniques as informed by opportunity reduction theory tend to predominate and have the most official and private-sector legitimacy in the crime prevention area. While ostensibly neutral in design, such techniques can have major consequences with regard to particular groups of people—usually the more marginalised such as the poor, the unemployed, indigenous people and young people. Often the intention of such approaches is to not only reduce the opportunities for crime (a technical objective), but to actually reduce the very presence and visibility of such groups in particular public spaces (a social and political objective). This is apparent, for example, in the use of police or private-security response teams to clear "undesirables" from affluent suburbs and commercial business premises.

For an exemplary exception to this kind of exclusionary approach, but one that shares many of its practical environmental modification concerns, we can refer to recent work that uses opportunity-reduction techniques to control drinking-related behaviour. For example, Homel and his colleagues (this volume) have been developing an intervention strategy aimed at reducing alcohol-related violence by changing the management methods of nightclubs. At one level, the approach can be seen as opportunity-reducing, since it lowers mass intoxication and improves informed regulation of licensees. At another level, however, it is clearly designed to increase and enhance the participation of young people, but in a safer environment. It thus has an inclusive, rather than exclusive, orientation.

Perspectives other than the conservative framework of crime prevention explicitly recognise and acknowledge the social nature of state and community intervention surrounding crime issues. For example, mainstream or liberal conceptions of crime prevention speak of deemphasising so-called "troublesome behaviour," and accentuating the positive and creative potential in people (Coventry et al., 1992). Crime prevention is thus linked to strategies of social development, that, in turn, require improvements in local material resources and capital infrastructures (e.g., schools, hospitals, public transport, job creation). Attempts are made to reduce the propensity to commit crime by enhancing the position of certain individuals and groups as participants in public life, users of public spaces and legitimate claimants on public resources. In some state jurisdictions, this has occasionally or periodically emerged as the favoured form of crime response (rather than a crime control focus). It is also linked to so-called "safer community" types of projects often coordinated by local councils.

In practical terms, both the liberal and radical perspectives agree that there needs to be a shift in thinking about crime prevention from being mainly about control and surveillance to crime prevention as supportive and developmental. Such a perspective can inform action taken on _specific issues_, as well as standing as a more _general principle of intervention_.

To illustrate the differences wrought in practice by application of principles derived from the different models of crime prevention, we can take the example of shopping centre security. A shopping centre today is much more than simply a gathering point for buyers and sellers of consumer items; it is an important point of social contact and social life for many different groups. In our hypothetical example, the problem is one of persistent vandalism and shoplifting. The solutions to this problem will vary, depending upon the political perspective of the crime prevention expert:

- The _conservative_ focus on opportunity reduction will translate into an increase in the number of security guards and in investment in security tags for merchandise, possibly restricting public transport to ensure a more affluent customer and a stepped-up use of spy cameras and store detectives.

• The *liberal* focus on opportunity enhancement might lead to the employment of youth and community workers within the shopping centre complex, the setting up of counseling and welfare services, and media campaigns designed to make people feel part of the "community" and to take pride in their shopping centre.

• The *radical* focus on social empowerment could see community action taken to contest the power of private owners and shopping centre managers to dictate the overall use and availability of the public space in the centre without consultation and direct community decision-making involvement.

We also need to be aware of how different perspectives, especially at points where there is an overlapping political agenda, can in fact *reinforce each other* at a practical level. A crime prevention concern to eliminate graffiti may attempt to reduce opportunity completely (via spray-proof paint-resistant surfaces), but not really get to the nub of the issue or the conditions that generate such activity. This more conservative crime-control type of approach, used in conjunction with efforts to displace random graffiti toward more structured graffiti projects (favoured by liberal "diversion" models), might well achieve a modicum of success. In this case, however, the focus on conventional crime, and thus fairly conventional crime prevention, does not preclude a radical social dimension. For instance, the channeling of graffiti work into projects such as painting bus shelters may have an additional function or consequence of combatting racism in a local area. That is, work done by local groups will often be protected by those groups, thus preventing racist and other anti-social slogans from being posted in these particular public places.

At this point, it needs to be emphasised as well that crime prevention operates at several *different levels of practical action*, from individual case measures through to political campaigns. These are not mutually exclusive. Indeed, efforts to enhance the well-being of specific communities and interest groups requires analysis of different levels of intervention (immediate and long-term; local, national, and international), and the adoption of a range of techniques, political alliances, and organisational methods.

CONCLUDING REMARKS

The intention of this paper has been to raise questions regarding the theoretical underpinnings and political orientations of much of what is accepted as "crime prevention" today. My focus has not been on explicating specific programs or working through particular concrete examples. Rather, the concern has been to comment generally on the ways in which adherence to certain ideological frameworks can be linked to both theoretical closure and the adoption of exclusionary practices. Contrary to this, it has been argued that the adoption of selected techniques, practices and methods does not make a particular program inherently good (or bad), or a success (or failure), or that the choice and use of these can somehow be separated from wider political issues.

The definition, orientation and strategic objectives of different crime prevention models is inherently and intractably political. Acknowledgement of the existence of competing perspectives (conservative, liberal and radical), and consequently diverse forms of intervention (some of which are mutually exclusive, others that reinforce each other), is important in sensitising us to the politics of our own practice, and in exposing the vested interests behind specific modes of crime prevention. Difficulties arise, however, when we unnecessarily conflate model with method, and fail to appreciate the contextual nature of practical crime prevention measures.

The impetus for this discussion came from the ways in which some of my students had responded to lectures on the different crime prevention models. Specifically, several were under the misapprehension that to be liberal or radical they could not refer to or use, for example, target hardening or other situational prevention measures. In other words, the model was to dominate the method. Against this narrow view, and also counter to the opposing idea that somehow practical projects can proceed without reference to the core ideas contained within the models, this paper has attempted to establish that crime prevention is first and foremost a *political process*. The manner in which particular programs or methods are constructed and used in practice always has important social and political implications.

Bearing this in mind, it is also important to have a vision of what we do that goes beyond that of "crime prevention" per se. That is, we need to continually assess the effects and implications of the different models and methods on the overall character of social life, and on the well-being of specific groups and communities. Stopping crime is always a possible project (at least theoretically) if only we had enough resources, tools and powers. But do we really want to create a kind of "surveillance state"— where we are all free from crime, but prisoners to our own security systems?

Crime prevention measures can and should have consequences that are oriented normatively, empirically and strategically toward creating a better society for all. In the light of increasingly rabid law-and-order discourse, and the tacit and express support for the crime control agenda by more conservative crime prevention practitioners, the task ahead for liberal and radical criminologists is to continue the fight against punitive, coercive forms of crime response. In doing so, there is a need to challenge the logic of conservatism, to build alliances between like-minded people and practitioners at an individual and organisational level, and to develop transitional strategies that incorporate any method of crime prevention that enhances and empowers people at local and regional levels.

To be clear about where we are going, we need to be certain about where we stand in the here and now. By separating out different political perspectives on crime prevention, and distinguishing these from the variety of specific methods and techniques available in this area, we are better able to situate the limits and possibilities of crime prevention as we head into the twenty-first century.

REFERENCES

Clarke, R. (ed.) (1992). *Situational Crime Prevention: Successful Case Studies*. Albany, NY: Harrow and Heston.

Coventry, G., J. Muncie and R. Walters (1992). *Rethinking Social Policy for Young People and Crime Prevention*. Discussion Paper No.1, National Centre for Socio-Legal Studies. Melbourne AUS: La Trobe University.

Cunneen, C. and R. White (1995). *Juvenile Justice: An Australian Perspective*. Melbourne, AUS: Oxford University Press.

Freund, J. (1969). *The Sociology of Max Weber*. New York, NY: Vintage Books.

Iadicola, P. (1986). "Community Crime Control Strategies." *Crime and Social Justice* 25:140-165.

McNamara, L. (1992). "Retrieving the Law and Order Issue from the Right: Alternative Strategies and Community Crime Prevention." *Law in Context* 10(1):91-122.

Sim, J., P. Scraton and P. Gordon (1987). "Introduction: Crime, the State and Critical Analysis." In: P. Scraton (ed.), *Law, Order and the Authoritarian State.* Milton Keynes, UK: Open University Press.

White, R. and A. Sutton (1995). "Crime Prevention, Urban Space and Social Exclusion." *Australian and New Zealand Journal of Sociology* 31(1):82-99.

White, R. and F. Haines (1996). *Crime and Criminology: An Introduction to Concepts and Explanations.* Melbourne, AUS: Oxford University Press.

Wilson, J. and G. Kelling (1982). "Broken Windows." *Atlantic Monthly* (March):29-38.

GUILT, SHAME AND SITUATIONAL CRIME PREVENTION

by

Richard Wortley

Griffith University

Abstract: This paper builds on Clarke and Homel's (in press) expansion of the situational crime prevention model, which includes new techniques for making the potential offender feel guilty or ashamed about their contemplated crime. In place of Clarke and Homel's single category of "inducing guilt or shame," two separate categories involving the manipulation of internal controls (guilt) and social controls (including shame) are proposed. The addition of these categories expands the repertoire of available crime prevention techniques by giving fuller recognition to the subtleties and complexities of the motivations to commit crime implicit in the rational choice perspective. It is argued that the new strategies also "soften" the narrow, target-hardening image of the situational approach, and may help researchers avoid counterproductive situational crime prevention effects.

In a recent revision of Clarke's (1992) classification of situational crime prevention techniques, Clarke and Homel (in press) have proposed the inclusion of additional strategies which "incorporate the threat of feeling guilty when contemplating a morally-wrong act and the fear of shame and embarrassment arising from the disapproval expressed by significant others when offending is revealed." Clarke and Homel have argued that the 12 categories of techniques included in the existing classification relied largely (though not entirely) on manipulations of physical costs and benefits. However, they pointed out, one of the main reasons people obey laws is their moral commitment to the legal code; law violation would generate significant psychological and social discomfiture. While it has been usual in criminology to think of moral commitment in developmental and dispositional terms (i.e., the product of early socialization), whether

Address correspondence to: Richard Wortley, School of Justice Administration, Griffith University, Brisbane 4111, Australia.

or not an individual invokes a moral rule on a given occasion often depends upon immediate contextual factors. Some situations facilitate rule evasion by allowing the individual to obscure the full criminal nature of the contemplated behavior. It follows that situational strategies can also be employed to strengthen the potential psychological and social costs of offending. According to Clarke and Homel, the development of strategies around offender guilt and shame has the potential to enhance the relevance of the situational crime prevention model by more fully reflecting "the richness and complexity of the rational choice perspective on crime."

Clarke and Homel's revised classification is shown in Table 1. To the existing three columns in Clarke's original classification table (which have been relabelled "increasing *perceived* effort," "increasing *perceived* risk," and "reducing *anticipated* rewards" to emphasise the perceptual basis of the model) they have added a fourth column which they have called "inducing guilt or shame." The strategies suggested under this category are "rule setting," "strengthening moral condemnation," "controlling disinhibitors," and "facilitating compliance." Rule setting involves reducing uncertainty about the impermissibility of a given behavior. For example, customs declarations that clearly specify what can and cannot be imported leave little room for potential offenders to exploit ambiguity in their own favor. Strengthening moral condemnation involves reinforcing the moral and social prohibitions against specific offences. For example, signs in shops announcing that "shoplifting is stealing" seek to counter the self-reassuring belief that shoplifting is not a "real" crime. Controlling disihibitors is concerned with minimizing conditions that impair the ability of individuals to critically self-evaluate their behavior. Restricting access to drugs and alcohol is the most obvious example of this strategy. Finally, facilitating compliance involves making it easier for individuals to follow rules. Thus, improving library check-out procedures denies potential book thieves the excuse that waiting in line was just too much trouble.

By highlighting the psychological and social dimensions implicit in the rational choice perspective, Clarke and Homel have opened exciting new directions for situational crime prevention. However, it is argued in this paper that the full potential of this expansion is not realised in the strategies provided in the revised classification. There are two main criticisms of the new fourth column. First, the list of suggested strategies for inducing guilt is by no means exhaustive. It will be shown that theories dealing with the moral reasoning of offenders that underpin these strategies have wider implications for crime prevention than are acknowledged by Clarke and Homel. Based on a reexamination of these theories, four alternative guilt-inducing strategies are proposed: "rule setting" (defined somewhat more broadly than the similarly-named category proposed by Clarke and Homel); "clarifying responsibility"; "clarifying consequences"; and "increasing victim worth."

Table 1: Clarke and Homel's Classification of Situational Crime Prevention Techniques

Increasing Perceived Effort	Increasing Perceived Risks	Reducing Anticipated Rewards	Inducing Guilt or Shame
Target hardening	Entry/exit screening	Target removal	Rule setting
Access control	Formal surveillance	Identifying property	Strengthening moral condemnation
Deflecting offenders	Surveillance by employees	Reducing temptation	Controlling disinhibitors
Controlling facilitators	Natural surveillance	Denying benefits	Facilitating compliance

Second, while Clarke and Homel are careful throughout their paper to talk about guilt *and* shame, their list of strategies does not clearly differentiate between these two phenomena. While guilt refers unambiguously to self-condemnation, shaming implies a mediating role for social condemnation. Indeed, Clarke and Homel recognised this problem and suggested that further work might lead to the separation of guilt and shame processes and the creation of a fifth column. This paper undertakes this task. Further, it will be argued that the threat of public condemnation is just one of a number of methods of situational behavioral control involving social influences. Four new situational crime prevention strategies based on the manipulation of social controls are described—"increasing social condemnation," "reducing social approval," "reducing imitation" and "crowd management."

EXPANDING STRATEGIES FOR INDUCING GUILT

In providing the theoretical rationale for their fourth column, Clarke
and Homel have examined the literature on offender rationalisation,
drawing particularly on Sykes and Matza's (1957) neutralization theory
and aspects of Bandura's (1976) social learning theory dealing with
"disengagement of self-deterring consequences" (p. 225). However, these
theories have been used by Clarke and Homel in a general way to justify
the move of situational crime prevention into the psychological domain,
rather than as the basis for the specific detail of the suggested crime
prevention strategies. Instead, the new strategies have been developed
largely through refinement of the existing classification system in order to
rectify imprecision identified through practical experience and experimentation in the crime prevention field. For example, the new strategy "controlling disinhibitors" was split off from the existing strategy of "controlling
facilitators." A consequence of this approach is that potentially useful
avenues for inducing guilt implicit in the work of Sykes and Matza and of
Bandura have been overlooked in the revised classification. The alternative approach suggested here is to derive strategies directly from the
theories.

The argument advanced in both neutralization and social learning
theories is that offenders are often able to avoid self-censure by cognitively
redefining crime situations in a way which minimizes their personal
culpability in their own eyes. Sykes and Matza suggested five specific
techniques of neutralization, and Bandura (1976; 1977) listed ten techniques of cognitive disengagement. These techniques are shown in Table
2, along with examples of accompanying cognitive distortions. It can be
seen that there is a great deal of similarity between the two groups of
techniques. Bandura (1977) further suggested that these techniques can
be grouped into four broad categories: those aimed at minimizing the
legitimacy of rule proscribing the behavior; those aimed at minimizing the
degree of personal responsibility for the behavior; those aimed at minimizing the negative consequences of the behavior; and those aimed at
minimizing the worth or blamelessness of the victim.

Bandura (1976) argued that the ability to engage in such mental
gymnastics often depends upon immediate environments and situations.
He clearly recognised the crime prevention potential of his work. Referring

Table 2: Comparison of Sykes and Matza (1957) and Bandura (1976, 1977)[1]

General Purpose	Sykes and Matza	Bandura	Examples
Minimizing the rule	Appeal to higher loyalties	Justification in terms of higher principles	"I had to steal to help a friend"
	Condemning the condemners		"The police are the real crooks"
		Palliative comparison	"At least I'm not a child-molester"
		Euphemistic labelling	"It's just tax minimization"
Minimizing personal responsibility	Denial of responsibility		"I was drunk and couldn't help myself
		Displacement of responsibility	"I was only doing what I was told"
		Diffusion of responsibility	"I was just part of a group"
Minimizing negative consequences	Denial of injury	Ignoring the consequences	"The shop was insured"
		Minimizing the consequences	"I just gave her a few slaps"
		Misconstruing the consequences	"She really enjoyed it"
Minimizing the victim	Denial of the victim	Dehumanizing the victim	"She was just a whore"
		Blaming the victim	"He deserved what he got"

[1]The format for this table was suggested by Ron Clarke and Ross Homel

to aggression, but raising implications for the control of anti-social behavior generally, he wrote:

> Given the variety of self-disinhibiting devices, a society cannot rely solely on individuals, however noble their convictions, to protect against brutal deeds. Just as aggression is not rooted in the individual, neither does its control reside solely there. Humanness requires, in addition to benevolent personal codes, safeguards built into social systems that uphold compassionate behavior and discourage cruelty (p. 227).

Table 2 suggests four broad situational crime prevention strategies for inducing guilt in potential offenders, corresponding to the four categories of guilt-minimization. The first is "rule setting." The strategy is based on the principle that offenders may seek to deny the essential wrongness of their actions, and may even claim the moral high ground, by contrasting their behavior with the more heinous behavior of others, focusing on the corruption of those in power, redefining their actions using more palatable language, or claiming to be serving a higher moral principle. The general crime prevention strategy involves reinforcing the illegitimacy of the targeted behavior. This strategy subsumes Clarke and Homel's "rule setting," but also overlaps their strategy of "strengthening moral condemnation." Whereas Clarke and Homel viewed "rule setting" largely in terms of clarifying the legal status of a behavior (e.g., harassment codes, customs declarations), here it includes reiteration of the fundamental moral imperative (e.g., "shoplifting is stealing" signs). However, the strategy does not include the public shaming techniques which Clarke and Homel suggest for "strengthening moral condemnation" (e.g., the "bloody idiot" campaign which attempts to utilize peer pressure to modify drinking-and-driving behavior), being concerned only with personal evaluations of wrongness. This distinction between self-condemnation and public condemnation is taken up again later in this paper.

The second strategy is "clarifying responsibility" for the behavior. This strategy is based on the principle that offenders may avoid self-blame for their actions by citing external causal agents, blaming others, employing disinhibitors, claiming a lack of behavioral alternatives, or using groups, organisations or superiors to obscure their personal contribution to anti-social acts. The general crime prevention strategy involves constructing situations that minimize disinhibition and reinforce personal agency. This category subsumes Clarke and Homel's "controlling disinhibitors" (e.g., server intervention) and "facilitating compliance" (e.g., improved library checkout) categories since both of these strategies seek to prevent offenders from blaming circumstances for their behavior. However, the scope is wider than this. For example, Bandura (1977) argued that the division of labor within organisations facilitates corruption by allowing individuals to hide behind a collective responsibility (as distinct from helping them avoid detection). Restructuring arrangements so that individuals perform discrete tasks forces them to take personal responsibility for their actions. Similarly, Zimbardo (1973) found that uniforms encourage a sense of collective identity in their wearers and weaken feelings of personal accountability. Zimbardo was originally interested in reducing the abuse of prisoners by prison officers, and argued that more informal modes of dress and the wearing of identifying name tags may help break down the sense of licence which anonymity and symbols of authority confer. Extending the principle, other applications may include controlling the wearing of gang "uniforms" in schools and other problem venues.

The third strategy is "clarifying consequences" of the proposed behavior. This strategy is based on the principle that offenders may seek to deny causing harm by portraying the outcome of their actions as being less serious than it really is, perhaps even denying that there is a victim. The general crime prevention strategy involves exposing offenders' attempts to gloss over the negative consequences of their behaviors. Health warnings on cigarette packets are an example of the use of this technique in the field of preventive medicine. This strategy is similar to Clarke and Homel's "strengthening moral condemnation," but differs in its emphasis on the outcome of the behavior rather than the ethical principle involved. Thus, rather than displaying signs equating shoplifting with stealing, the signs employing this strategy would emphasize the costs of shoplifting to the community. Using this principle, copyright messages on compact disks, computer software, videos and so forth emphasize the detrimental effects of piracy to the entertainment industry, and quarantine signs at airports and borders attempt to raise the consciousness (and conscience) of travellers about the possible devastation to local agriculture caused by importing undeclared foodstuffs and animal products. Also in this category are road-side signs warning about the effects of speeding and drinking and driving, and those indicating accident "black-spots."

The fourth strategy is "increasing victim worth." This strategy is based on the principle that people find it easier to victimize those who can be stereotyped as sub-human or unworthy, those who can be portrayed as deserving of the fate which has befallen them, or even those who are simply outsiders or anonymous. The general crime prevention strategy involves creating environments and devising situations that minimize depersonalization and strengthen the emotional attachment between potential offenders and victims. This strategy is a rich source of crime prevention techniques largely ignored in Clarke and Homel's revised classification. Victim-offender conciliation programs, while not strictly crime prevention (since they occur after the fact), utilize the principle that it is more difficult to offend against people who have been invested with personal qualities (Launay, 1987). Investigating victim-offender relationships at the crime scene, Indermaur (1994, and in this volume) found that the offering of resistance during a robbery often had the effect of arousing "righteous indignation" in the offender. Indermaur suggests that victims need to adopt non-confrontational techniques in order to avoid providing "justification" for the offender to resort to violence. Appearance, dress and mannerisms may also facilitate the process of depersonalization and increase chances of victimisation. For example, Zimbardo (1973) showed that the wearing of uniforms and badges of outgroup membership by victims encouraged their stereotyping by aggressors. Dehumanisation may be further facilitated by the physical environments in which potential victims are located. The finding that victimisation rates are high in large housing estates and run-down ghettos (Newman, 1973; Pease, 1992) may be partly explained by the ease with which inhabitants of these environments are rendered anonymous and devoid of personal qualities.

The principle of reducing the opportunities for offenders to derogate their intended targets may be extended to include property or organisations as victims. Urban renewal and other environmental beautification programs may be successful crime prevention strategies not just because they increase the commitment of residents to guardianship (Fowler and Mangione, 1986; Lavrakas and Kushmuk, 1986; LeBeau, 1987), but also because they make it cognitively more difficult for offenders to justify vandalism and other crimes by removing the excuse that the area is rundown in any case. In a similar vein, prisoners are less likely to damage prison property when fittings are of good quality and a sense of territoriality over living areas is encouraged (Atlas and Dunham, 1990). Employee share schemes, incentive schemes and general attention to reducing job dissatisfaction may increase in employees a sense of attachment to a company and inhibit their ability to portray the company in ways that justify acting fraudulently against it (Johnson, 1987; O'Block et al., 1991).

SHAME AND OTHER SOCIAL INFLUENCES

Shame is a complex concept in that it implies a degree of self-reproach (Grasmick and Bursik, 1990) that is often brought about by social condemnation (Braithwaite, 1989). However, there are sound theoretical reasons for disentangling the internal and social components of shame. A number of sociological and psychological perspectives support this distinction. Recent theorising in the deterrence literature has centered on expanding the notion of expected utility of criminal behavior beyond conventional consideration of state-imposed sanctions (Grasmick and Bursik, 1990; Williams and Hawkins, 1986). Specifically, these developments have emphasised the roles of both internalized norms and attachment to significant others as sources of potential punishment that need to be incorporated into the general deterrence model. Learning or behavioral theories have made similar distinctions. Traditionally, learning theorists have held that human behavior is regulated by its physical determinants (tangible rewards and punishments). However, social learning theory (Bandura, 1976, 1977) broadened the notion of the regulating consequences of behavior to include social determinants (praise and condemnation of others) and self-generated determinants (self-judgements of performance assessed against personal standards of behavior). Neutralizations or cognitive disengagements, then, are conceptualised as the selective activation of self-generated determinants.

Perhaps the distinction between guilt and shame is most clearly made in moral development theory (Kohlberg, 1976). This approach has fitted physical, social and personal controls on behavior into a developmental hierarchy of moral reasoning. In the pre-conventional stage of development, moral decisions are made in relation to the avoidance of physical punishment. In the conventional stage, the concern is primarily with appearing "nice" in the eyes of others. The post-conventional stage involves decisions of conscience. According to Kohlberg, behavior controlled by social reactions involves a lower order of reasoning than behavior controlled by self-evaluation (and behavior controlled by physical means is lower still). An explicit tenet of the hierarchical approach, then, is that one can be sensitive to the opinions of others without feeling any personal sense of having done wrong.

The clearest example of the confound between guilt and shame in Clarke and Homel's revised classification is in their strategy of "increasing moral condemnation." As already noted, the techniques they suggest for this strategy involve both increasing self-condemnation ("shoplifting is stealing" signs) and subjecting the potential offender to public criticism (the "bloody idiot" drunk-driving campaign). Other techniques suggested in this category are ambiguous. The use of roadside speedometers is a technique to induce guilt when only the driver is made aware of the result; it is a method of shaming when other drivers are also made aware of the result.

In place of Clarke and Homel's "increasing moral condemnation," the strategy "increasing social condemnation" is suggested to more precisely capture the public criticism and embarrassment components of shaming. A number of specific techniques for increasing anticipated social condemnation have already been mentioned. There are undoubtedly others. While it addresses the lower end of the "crime" scale (and is possibly even apocryphal), the use of urine-sensitive swimming-pool dyes exemplifies the concept of utilizing the threat of public exposure to modify behavior. The prospect of suffering humiliation is also the basis of signs in shops depicting the social stigma associated with being caught shoplifting. An alternative approach is to persuade those affected by crime to be more vociferous in their condemnation of offenders. Brantingham (1986) reports a study showing that when school repair costs were taken from that school's film budget, peer pressure on offenders resulted in a significant reduction in vandalism. Elements of social embarrassment can also be found in existing strategies. Merchandise tags ("entry/exit screening") that set off clamorous alarms draw public attention as well as alerting security staff to a theft. Similarly, the success of "natural surveillance" and "surveillance by employees" may partly depend upon the fact that illegal behavior will be viewed and condemned by others.

Situational social influence, however, is not restricted to fear of condemnation. In some cases illegal behavior can be socially rewarded. This occurs particularly within delinquent subcultures (Bandura, 1976). Thus, an additional strategy under the category of social controls is "reducing social approval" for illegal acts. The most obvious way to operationalize this strategy is through controlling the opportunities for offenders to reinforce one another. Crime and violence within schools may be reduced

by altering patterns of contact and interaction among members of delinquent cliques (Hawkins and Lishner, 1987). Parents employ a similar
principle of structuring social reinforcements when they screen their
children's associates (Le Blanc, 1995). Limiting the extent to which other
members of the subculture become aware of a delinquent act may also
reduce opportunities for social reinforcement. Clarke and Homel's suggested technique of rapid cleaning of graffiti, which they give as an example
of "denying benefits," may be more appropriately listed under this strategy,
since many of the benefits for the graffitist are reaped in increased
subcultural status (Sloan-Howitt and Kelling, 1992). The decision by
television stations (in Australia at least) not to broadcast "streaking" and
other field invasions by spectators at sporting events also aims to contain
the reinforcing publicity that such behavior attracts.

Social condemnation and approval are consequent determinants of
behavior, that is, they are situational crime prevention strategies inas-
much as they can be manipulated to alter the anticipated social outcomes
for criminal acts. Bandura (1977) has made the point that behavior is also
under the control of antecedent determinants that act as situational
instigators for action. One such social cue to engage in behavior is the
observation of someone else performing that behavior, particularly when
the actor is of high status or is respected by the observer. For example, a
pedestrian (especially one who is well dressed) crossing the street against
a red light will readily induce others to follow (Lefkowitz et al., 1955). This
suggests that an important addition to existing situational crime prevention strategies is "reducing imitation." The general strategy involves
exposing potential offenders to prosocial models or reducing the opportunity for potential offenders to imitate others performing antisocial acts.
Supervisors, then, can reduce employee fraud or other forms of corruption
by setting high and conspicuous standards of probity for subordinates
(O'Block et al., 1991). Conveniently, models need not appear in-person.
The principle that people will imitate models underpins public education
campaigns (litter reduction, seat-belt wearing, etc.) that enlist the en-
dorsement of celebrities, and also provides the rationale for restricting or
censoring media portrayals of pornography and violence (Lab, 1992).
(Although, arguably, both of these measures only qualify as situational
crime prevention if they are carried out near the site of potential crimes).
In many cases it is the observed result of illegal behavior which provides
the model rather than observation of the act itself. Cleaning of graffiti not
only denies the offender social rewards, but also removes the inducement

for others to imitate his or her feats. A similar explanation can be applied to the finding that rapid repair of vandalism inhibits further vandalism (Challinger, 1992). Attempts can also be made to neutralize or discredit antisocial models. Kallis and Varnier (1985) recommended that the most effective anti-shoplifting signs are "Make a choice on your own—don't shoplift," which are designed to help potential offenders withstand the effects of peer influence.

The final suggested strategy involving social controls is "crowd management." That individuals behave differently when in the presence of others than when alone is social psychology's *raison d'etre*. Like models, crowds can act as situational instigators of behavior. Specifically, crowds are associated with two broad psychological processes relevant to criminal behavior. First, belonging to a crowd can cause members to deindividuate—to submerge their identities within the group—resulting in their decreased ability to self-monitor their behavior and permitting them to engage in acts that they would ordinarily not perform (Prentice-Dunn and Rogers, 1989; Zimbardo, 1969). Deindividuation is commonly associated with mob violence (Colman, 1991). Second, being crowded—subjected to high density conditions— can cause individuals to suffer increased stress, anxiety and frustration, which can trigger hostility and aggression (Paulus and Nagar, 1989). For example, crowding has been shown to be related to levels of urban crime (Gove et al., 1979), disciplinary infractions in prisons (Cox et al., 1984) and nightclub disturbances (Macintyre and Homel, in press; Ramsay, 1986).

Deindividuation is a form of psychological disinhibition and as such has already been dealt with under the strategy of "clarifying responsibility." "Crowd management," then, is concerned here largely with the problem of crowding. At its simplest level, reducing crowding involves either reducing the number of people in a given environment, or increasing the available space for those people. The most obvious way for establishments to reduce crowding is to set lower limits to patron numbers. This type of strategy is well established in the crime prevention literature. The concept of entry controls to reduce congestion is a feature of crime prevention through environmental design (Newman, 1973), and is also covered to some extent in the "deflecting offenders" category in Clarke and Homel's classification. However, crowd management is broader than this. The experience of crowding involves a perceptual dimension, and so the crowding effects can be moderated by a number of social and architectural features in the environment (Paulus and Nagar, 1989). For example, positive mood states and efficient room design can reduce the effects of social density, while windows and high ceilings can increase the sense of spaciousness. Thus, disorder has been found to be lower in nightclubs that create a relaxing ambience (Ramsay, 1986). Similarly, Macintyre and Homel (in press) found that nightclub violence was reduced by floor plans that regulated traffic flow and minimized unnecessary jostling. Given this expanded view of crowd management, creation of a separate category seems warranted.

Table 3: Proposed Fourth and Fifth Columns of Situational Techniques

Increasing Social Controls	Inducing Guilt
Increasing social condemnation: "bloody idiot" campaign enlisting support of victims public roadside speedometer	*Rule setting:* harassment codes customs declarations "shoplifting is stealing" signs
Reducing social approval: dispersing school gangs screening children's associates non-televising of "streaking"	*Clarifying responsibility:* server intervention assigning discrete tasks limiting uniform use
Reducing imitation: rapid repair of vandalism discrediting models supervisors as exemplars	*Clarifying consequences:* copyright messages quarantine warning signs accident "black-spot" warnings
Crowd management: limiting patron density creating pleasant club ambience regulating patron flow	*Increasing victim worth:* victim cooperation strategies avoiding outgroup insignia environmental beautification

The two separate columns suggested to replace Clarke and Homel's single category of "inducing guilt and shame" column are shown in Table 3.

CONCLUSIONS: "HARD" AND "SOFT" SITUATIONAL PREVENTION

According to Clarke (1992), situational crime prevention "relies... not upon improving society or its institutions, but simply upon reducing opportunities for crime" (p. 3). Criticisms of the situational model have typically dwelt on the target-hardening aspects of opportunity reduction. Such measures have been portrayed as narrow and simplistic responses to crime that take insufficient account of offender motivations (Trasler, 1986). Moreover, concerns have been raised about the social implications of the unfettered application of target-hardening principles (Bottoms, 1990; Grabosky, 1994, and in this volume; Weiss, 1987). Taken to its logical conclusion, so the argument goes, situational crime prevention engenders public fear and distrust, and encourages the development of a siege mentality. Not only is this vision of society unappealing, a reliance on target-hardening can produce effects opposite to those sought. Walls, guards, conspicuous security devices and the like divide rather than build communities by separating and isolating their members. At some point, then, situational crime prevention runs the danger of becoming counter-productive, creating the very social conditions which foster criminal behavior.

These attacks on the situational model have not gone unchallenged (Clarke, 1992). Even so, the developments proposed in Clarke and Homel (in press), and expanded upon in this paper, help to "soften" the hard-edged, "locks-and-bolts" image of situational crime prevention by forcing a wider interpretation of opportunity reduction. The explicit recognition of the role of psychological and social "opportunities" to commit crime suggests a range of new, often less obtrusive ways of countering criminal behavior at the situational level. These "soft" strategies rely on providing immediate moral and social support to the prospective offender, and may be readily contrasted with the more usual "hard" constraining techniques of situational prevention.

Presented with alternative "hard" and "soft" situational prevention strategies, researchers and practitioners may need to make careful decisions about the appropriate approach for a given crime problem. For some offenders, "soft" approaches may be quite ineffective. Kohlberg's work on moral development suggests that pre-conventional moral reasoners are essentially motivated by external rewards and punishments, and will be largely unmoved by social pressure or appeals to their conscience. Thus, while attempts by victims to elicit pity might deter some rapists, other rapists will be deaf to such pleas and may even be further aroused by them (Cohen et al., 1971). On the other hand, techniques designed to induce guilt and social embarrassment may prove particularly useful for crimes involving relatively uncommitted offenders, such as those involved in minor acts of juvenile delinquency, and white-collar crimes, where the offender can be assumed to have a considerable stake in conformity.

More interestingly, in some cases "hard" and "soft" approaches might suggest contradictory solutions. Opposing philosophies of prison design offer a good example this. Using conventional target-hardening techniques, prison officers can be protected from possible assaults from inmates by the installation of bars and bullet-proof glass, and by the use of technology such as automatic doors that minimize the need for personal contact between the two groups (Atlas and Dunham, 1990). Yet these strategies also serve to facilitate the process of depersonalization, which may make officers cognitively more acceptable targets for assault should the opportunity arise. The alternative strategy is to reduce the physical barriers separating inmates and staff, and encourage greater interpersonal contact between the two groups. Ultimately, officers may well be safer in an environment in which they are known and treated as individuals by the inmates (and *vice versa*). The extent to which this principle can be applied more generally is problematic. For example, providing security screens for taxi drivers appears to have been relatively successful and to have produced few apparent side effects (Chaiken et al., 1992). Nevertheless, the expanded situational model provides a starting point for analysing the unintended psychological and social impact of target-hardening measures, and may help researchers strike the balance between appropriate opportunity reduction and a "fortress society."

Acknowledgements: The author wishes to thank Ron Clarke and Ross Homel for their valuable comments on an earlier draft of this paper.

REFERENCES

Atlas, R.I. and R.G. Dunham (1990). "Changes in Prison Facilities as a Function of Correctional Philosophy." In: J.W. Murphy and J.E. Dison (eds.), *Are Prisons Any Better? Twenty Years of Correctional Reform*. Newbury Park, CA: Sage.

Bandura, A. (1976). "Social Learning Analysis of Aggression." In: E. Ribes-Inesta and A. Bandura (eds.), *Analysis of Delinquency and Aggression*. Hillsdale, NJ: Lawrence Erlbaum.

—— (1977). *Social Learning Theory*. Englewood Cliffs, NJ: Prentice-Hall.

Bottoms, A.E. (1990). "Crime Prevention Facing the 1990s." *Policing and Society*, 1:3-22.

Braithwaite, J. (1989). *Crime, Shame and Reintegration*. Cambridge, UK: Cambridge University Press.

Brantingham, P. (1986). "Trends in Canadian Crime Prevention." In: K. Heal and G. Laycock (eds.), *Situational Crime Prevention: From Theory into Practice*. London, UK: Her Majesty's Stationery Office

Chaiken, J.M., M.W. Lawless and K.A. Stevenson (1992). "Exact Fares on Buses." In: R.V Clarke (ed.), *Situational Crime Prevention: Successful Case Studies*. Albany, NY: Harrow and Heston.

Challinger, D. (1992). "Less Telephone Vandalism: How Did it Happen?" In: R.V. Clarke (ed.), *Situational Crime Prevention: Successful Case Studies*. Albany, NY: Harrow and Heston.

Clarke, R.V. (1992). "Introduction." In: R.V Clarke (ed.), *Situational Crime Prevention: Successful Case Studies*. Albany, NY: Harrow and Heston.

—— and R. Homel (in press). "A Revised Classification of Situational Crime Prevention Techniques." In: S.P. Lab (ed.), *Crime Prevention at the Crossroads*. Cincinnati, OH: Anderson.

Cohen, M.L., R. Garafalo, R. Boucher and T. Seghorn (1971). "The Psychology of Rapists." *Seminars in Psychiatry* 3:307-327.

Colman, A. (1991). "Psychological Evidence in South African Murder Trials." *The Psychologist* November:482-486.

Cox, V.C., P.B. Paulus and G. McCain (1984). "Prison Crowding Research: The Relevance for Prison Housing Standards and a General Approach Regarding Crowding Phenomena." *American Psychologist*, 39:1148-1160.

Fowler, F.J. and T.W. Mangione (1986). "A Three-Pronged Effort to Reduce Crime and Fear of Crime: The Hartford Experiment." In D.P. Rosenbaum (ed.), *Community Crime Prevention. Does it Work?* Beverly Hills, CA: Sage.

Gove, G.W., M. Hughs and O.R. Gale (1979). "Overcrowding in the Home: An Empirical Investigation of its Possible Pathological Consequences." *American Sociological Review* 44:59-80.

Grabosky, P.N. (1994). "Counterproductive Crime Prevention." In: *Proceedings of the Centre for Crime Policy and Public Safety Crime Prevention Conference*. Brisbane, AUS: Griffith University.

Grasmick, H.G. and R.J. Bursik (1990). "Conscience, Significant Others and Rational Choice." *Law and Society Review* 34:837-861.

Hawkins, J.D. and D.M. Lishner (1987). "Schooling and Delinquency." In: E.H. Johnson (ed.), *Handbook on Crime and Delinquency Prevention.* New York, NY: Greenwood Press.

Indermaur, D. (1994). "Reducing the Opportunities for Violence in Robbery and Property Crime: The Perspectives of Offenders and Victims." In: *Proceedings of the Centre for Crime Policy and Public Safety Crime Prevention Conference.* Brisbane, AUS: Griffith University.

Johnson, E.H. (1987). "Prevention in Business and Industry." In: E.H. Johnson (ed.), *Handbook on Crime and Delinquency Prevention.* New York, NY: Greenwood Press.

Kallis, M.J. and D.J. Varnier (1985). "Consumer Shoplifting: Orientations and Deterrents." *Journal of Criminal Justice* 13:470.

Kohlberg, L. (1976). "Moral Stages and Moralization." In: T. Likona (ed.), *Moral Development and Behavior.* New York, NY: Holt, Rinehart and Winston.

Lab, S.P. (1992). *Crime Prevention: Approaches, Practices and Evaluations* (2nd ed.). Cincinnati, OH: Anderson.

Launay, G. (1987). "Victim-Offender Conciliation. In: B.J. McGurk, D.M. Thornton and M. Williams (eds.), *Applying Psychology to Imprisonment.* London, UK: Her Majesty's Stationery Office.

Lavrakas, P.J. and J.W. Kushmuk (1986). "Evaluating Crime Prevention Through Environmental Design: The Portland Commercial Demonstration Project." In: D.P. Rosenbaum (ed.), *Community Crime Prevention. Does it Work?* Beverly Hills, CA: Sage.

LeBeau, J.L. (1987). "Environmental Design as a Rationale for Prevention." In: E.H. Johnson (ed.), *Handbook on Crime and Delinquency Prevention.* New York, NY: Greenwood Press.

Le Blanc, M. (1995). "Common, Temporary and Chronic Delinquency. Prevention Strategies During Compulsory School." In: P.H. Wikstrom, R.V. Clarke. and J. McCord (eds.), *Integrating Crime Prevention Strategies: Propensity and Opportunity.* Stockholm, SWE: National Council for Crime Prevention.

Lefkowitz, M., R.R. Blake and J.S. Mouton (1955). "Status Factors in Pedestrian Violation of Traffic Signals." *Journal of Abnormal and Social Psychology* 51:704-705.

Macintyre, S. and R. Homel (in press). "Danger on the Dance Floor. A Study of Interior Design, Crowding and Aggression in Nightclubs." *Crime Prevention Studies,* vol. 7.

Newman, O. (1973). *Defensible Space: Crime Prevention Through Urban Design.* New York, NY: Collier.

O'Block, R.L., J.F. Donnermeyer and S.E. Doeren (1991). *Security and Crime Prevention* (2nd ed.). Boston, MA: Butterworth-Heinemann.

Paulus, P.B. and D. Nagar (1989). "Environmental Influences on Groups." In P.B. Paulus (ed.), *Psychology of Group Influence* (2nd ed.). Hillsdale, NJ: Lawrence Erlbaum.

Pease, K. (1992). "Preventing Burglary on a British Public Housing Estate." In: R.V. Clarke (ed.), *Situational Crime Prevention: Successful Case Studies*. Albany, NY: Harrow and Heston.

Prentice-Dunn, S. and R.W. Rogers (1989). "Deindividuation." In: P.B. Paulus (ed.), *Psychology of Group Influence* (2nd ed.). Hillsdale, NJ: Lawrence Erlbaum.

Ramsay, M. (1986). "Preventing Disorder." In: K. Heal and G. Laycock (eds.), *Situational Crime Prevention: From Theory into Practice*. London, UK: Her Majesty's Stationery Office.

Sloan-Howitt, M. and G.L. Kelling (1992). "Subway Graffiti in New York City: 'Gettin up' vs. 'meanin it and cleanin it.'" In: R.V. Clarke (ed.), *Situational Crime Prevention: Successful Case Studies*. Albany, NY: Harrow and Heston.

Sykes, G. and D. Matza (1957). "Techniques of Neutralization: A Theory of Delinquency." *American Journal of Sociology* 22:664-670.

Trasler, G. (1986). "Situational Crime Control and Rational Choice: A Critique." In: K. Heal and G. Laycock (eds.), *Situational Crime Prevention: From Theory into Practice*. London, UK: Her Majesty's Stationery Office.

Weiss, R.P. (1987). "The Community and Prevention." In: E.H. Johnson (ed.), *Handbook on Crime and Delinquency Prevention*. New York, NY: Greenwood Press.

Williams, K.R. and R. Hawkins (1986). "Perceptual Research on General Deterrence: A Critical Review." *Law and Society Review* 20:545-72.

Zimbardo, P.G. (1969). "The Human Choice: Individuation, Reason, and Order, vs Deindividuation, Impulse, and Chaos." *Nebraska Symposium on Motivation* 17:237-307.

—— (1973). "The Psychological Power and Pathology of Imprisonment." In: E. Aronson and R. Helmreich (eds.), *Social Psychology*. New York, NY: Van Nostrand.

REDUCING THE OPPORTUNITIES FOR VIOLENCE IN ROBBERY AND PROPERTY CRIME: THE PERSPECTIVES OF OFFENDERS AND VICTIMS

by

David Indermaur

University of Western Australia

Abstract: This paper reports on research undertaken in Western Australia in 1993 on violence associated with robbery and property crime. Firsthand accounts from 88 offenders and 10 victims are examined for information and perspectives that may be relevant to the prevention of such violence. Results suggest that violence occurring in the course of a robbery or a property crime is most effectively prevented by reducing the overall rate of these crimes. However, once an offender has confronted a victim, the victim's behaviour may be critical in preventing violence. Appreciating that offenders may be very afraid or even angry with the victim suggests a non-confrontational approach and one that may even facilitate the offender's escape.

INTRODUCTION

Stories regularly appearing in our newspapers of robbery and burglary victims being "senselessly" bashed by offenders cause great alarm in the community. Despite the terror associated with these events, only a small proportion of property crimes actually involve encounters between victims and offenders. This paper explores the prevalence and nature of violence

Address correspondence to: David Indermaur, Crime Research Centre, University of Western Australia, 14 Parkway, Nedlands, Western Australia 6907.

associated with robbery and property crime, and how the risks of such violence may be minimised.

The first approach to reducing violence associated with property crime is to reduce the likelihood that an encounter with an offender will occur at all. As Cook (1985) demonstrates, the number of violent robberies remains a constant proportion of the total number of robberies in the U.S., and, therefore, the most effective way of preventing violence associated with robbery is to prevent robbery in general. The general prevention of crime through routine precautions will be discussed in the final section of this paper.

The second approach to preventing violence in property crime focuses on the confrontation between the victim and offender. In a robbery the confrontation can be planned by the offender, and generally robbers appear to avoid violence by achieving the consent of the victim through threats. However, phenomenological studies of robbery suggest that many robbers are motivated by the sense of power and dominance that the event offers (Katz, 1988). This may help explain why the literature on victim resistance is somewhat equivocal regarding the relationship between victim resistance and violence (see Cook, 1985, 1986, 1987). For example, Cook (1986) points out that in many cases of robbery resulting in victim injury, victims were resisting not to protect their property but because they believed that the offender(s) was about to use violence.

Cook (1986) discusses the problems in interpreting the available data on victim resistance:

> Since we cannot distinguish between the influence of the robber's actions on the victim's response and the influence of the victim's actions on the robber's response, we are left simply not knowing how to interpret the statistical patterns of association between resistance and injury [p.414].

However, it is clear that robbery injuries are more likely to occur where the offender does not have a gun (e.g., see New South Wales Bureau of Crime Statistics and Research, 1987). Presumably the presence of a weapon obviates the need for any other display of dominance and will, as the weapon provides compelling support for the threat of force. Harding and Blake's (1989) study suggests that robbers choose weapons that appear intimidating as part of their "victim management strategy." Accounts of robbers (e.g., Gabor et al., 1987) suggest that the presence of a weapon is likely to make the offender more confident and the victim less likely to resist.

The "managed robbery" can be contrasted with the sudden and unplanned confrontations between victims and offenders that sometimes occur in burglaries and car thefts. These confrontations are quite dangerous for the victim for a number of reasons. First, it is likely that the offender will not feel in control. Second, in the confusion the victim may be more likely to confront or resist the offender. Third, without a weapon the offender may not have any means to exert his or her will other than through the use of violence.

There are some robberies where violence is actually planned by offenders as a means of initiating the robbery. Muggings, as Katz (1988) points out, may actually represent a more immature form of robbery. Muggers may assault the victim to begin with because they anticipate the victim's resistance or do not trust their own abilities to manage the robbery. Katz (1988) points out that a mugging is the easiest form of robbery. By contrast, a "stick up" (threatening to use force) requires the offender to "face down" a victim. The skill of facing down, that is, using language and personal "presence" to "front" and threaten a victim, is often built on the knowledge that the offender *can* use violence if necessary. This skill or confidence is best gained through past experiences of robbery where violence was actually used (as in a "mugging"). In other words, for youths who may feel afraid of confronting a victim, attacking a victim from behind in a gang requires not only less courage but also less skill.

Another dimension to the problem of understanding victim-offender confrontation arises where a male property offender confronts a female victim. In these circumstances a different form of violence—sexual violence—may emerge. Warr (1988) argues that residential rapes committed by strangers and burglary are both crimes of "stealth" and have similar opportunity structures. Thus, the characteristics that make a dwelling attractive to a burglar will also appeal to a rapist. Households containing only one female adult are at risk because they present an easy target for both rape and burglary (not well-protected, no witnesses and confined space that is easier to take and manage control of).

Warr (1988) supports his argument with two pieces of evidence. First, a relatively high ($r = 0.79$) correlation is observed between rates of burglary and rape in 155 jurisdictions of the U.S. in 1980. Second, the sociodemographic variables associated with burglary also largely exist for rape based on 1980 U.S. census data ($r = 0.99$). The correlation between the associated demographic factors is even higher than exists between aggravated assault and homicide. Controlling for the opportunity variables significantly reduces the correlation between rape and burglary, pointing to the importance of these variables.

Warr (1988) is thus arguing that home-intrusion rape (rape by a stranger-intruder in the victim's home) is a product of the opportunity structures of both rape and burglary. Some rape/burglaries will occur as an offender intent on one crime takes the opportunity to commit the other; however, the associations, Warr argues, come about because residences that present a target to burglars independently also present a target to rapists.

In a property crime, if the offender has switched his intention from theft (of property) to sex the issue of victim resistance becomes more complex. Grace (1993) provides a review of the literature on the value of physical resistance to sexual assault. Generally, studies in this area have found that verbal rather than physical resistance is more effective in preventing the completion of a sexual assault. However, Grace notes that the results are equivocal and that much depends on the location of the attack and other dynamics. But Grace (1993) does conclude that "all the research suggests that resistance does not result in an increase in severe injury" (p.23). Injury-free successful resistance seems most likely if the victim can escape before the violence escalates.

Apart from studying the interactional dynamics of the victim-offender encounter, there are a number of other factors specifically associated with offender psychology that can help explain why violence may sometimes occur in the course of a property crime. In particular, there are a number of studies that focus on how men who become violent perceive the nature of social interactions, construct meanings and calculate their options. These studies suggest that the perceptual field that many offenders enter the property crime scene with may have already tipped the balance in favour of violence.

The key problem stems from the calculation by the offender that violence is "necessary." This calculation appears to be the outcome of several cognitive distortions, common amongst violent men, which have been articulated by Novaco and Welsh (1989). First, they argue that being generally angry disposes a person to see aggression everywhere in much the same way that a hungry person sees food everywhere (this process is referred to by Novaco and Welsh as "attentional cueing"). The tendency of offenders to perceive hostility (hostile attributional bias) has been well documented in a series of studies (e.g. Dodge et al., 1990; Driscoll, 1982).

Second, Novaco and Welsh (1989) point out that the more someone has been exposed to aggression, the more readily he or she will perceive aggression. For example, Shelly and Toch (1968) found that prisoners with histories of violence were more likely to pick up violent scenes in an ambiguous situation than prisoners with non-violent histories ("perceptual matching"). Wolfgang and Ferracuti's (1967) theory of the subculture of violence is also based on the notion that exposure to violence will have the effect of normalising the use of violence.

Third, Novaco and Welsh (1989) argue that violent people are more likely to see the behaviour of their victim preceding the assault as a result of a natural aggressiveness of the victim rather than a product of their (the victim's) fear ("attribution error"). Fourth, those who regularly or unnecessarily engage in violence are likely to be deficient in their ability to adopt alternative roles, and tend to think that they have no alternative but to respond violently ("false consensus"). This point is supported by the findings of Short and Simeonsson (1986), who found that delinquents have an underdeveloped ability to see a situation from different perspectives.

Finally, Novaco and Welsh (1989) argue that the tendency to continue to believe one's first impression concerning the other's intentions rather than adjusting it as the situation changes (anchoring effect) is a cognitive distortion relevant to violent behaviour. This tendency is maximised by high arousal such as anger or fear, which tends to block the incorporation of information that may correct the offender's original impression.

Novaco and Welsh's (1989) explanation of violence provides a valuable perspective on understanding why, contrary to common sense, an offender may perpetrate violence in the course of a property crime. For example, an offender engaged in a property crime when confronted by a victim may perceive the victim's actions as malevolent and, due to the anchoring effect and/or his high arousal, be unable to revise this perception of threat. The perception of malevolence will be maintained by the offender, even though the victim may be more afraid than the offender. This may help explain why in the situation where a car owner approaches a group of offenders in the act of stealing his car the offenders may attack the owner rather than take flight. According to the preceding discussion it is because the offender: is already angry; will perceive the owner's actions as aggressive; and considers the only appropriate (manly) response to be "fight fire with fire" and "get in first." Even if the owner says "I don't want to hurt you," it is unlikely that the offender would believe him or her. Morrison (1993) provides a good example of the value of Novaco and Welsh's (1989) analysis:

> Offenders often claimed to have interpreted their victims' actions as challenging, or threatening. But, in only a few cases did the victims appreciate that their actions might have appeared threatening to the offender. Most were left puzzled over what had sparked off the on-slaught [p.29].

The likelihood of the offender attacking the owner is also heightened if the offender is in a group, not only because the group provides the necessary strength to overcome the victim but also because the psycho-logical stakes are higher. As Morrison (1993) found, although offenders will dismiss the importance of the peer-group audience, victims of the same incidents see the effect of the audience as significant in most cases.

The foregoing discussion suggests a number of ways in which violence may occur in the course of a victim-offender confrontation. Although there has been considerable discussion of robbery violence, there have been few studies of why offenders involved in a property crime use violence. This paper reports on work conducted in Western Australia that attempted to explore this question by talking directly to offenders. This analysis is supplemented by interviews with victims of violence about how they perceived the situation. The term "violent property crime" is used to describe situations where a property crime (including robbery) is associated with actual violence.

Before looking at offenders' and victims' accounts, it is important to gain some perspective on the extent of violence associated with property crime. The discussion about preventive measures needs to be placed squarely in the context that most people (including offenders) want to avoid violence. It will be argued that more violence can be prevented by studying how most violence is naturally avoided.

THE LIKELIHOOD OF VIOLENCE IN PROPERTY CRIME

The major property offences where a victim may confront an offender are robbery, burglary and car theft. In Western Australia, with a popula-tion of 1,657,500 in 1992, there were 51,384 burglaries, 824 robberies and 17,243 vehicle thefts reported to the police. These figures significantly underestimate the true extent of these crimes in the community because many victims don't report crimes to the police. The 1993 Australian Bureau of Statistics (ABS) victimisation survey (ABS, 1994) provides an indication of the extent of underreporting. Using the survey results as a guide we can estimate that in Western Australia in 1992 there was a total of approximately 101,544 burglaries, robberies and vehicle thefts (indicating that for the offences combined the reporting rate was 68%). The main reason given by victims for not reporting the offence to the police, particularly in regard to robbery—the crime most likely to result in injury—was that the event was trivial (ABS, 1994). Therefore the crimes reported to the police largely represent the more serious two-thirds of offences committed. Yet police have records of only 433 cases in 1992 where victims of robbery or property crime sustained any injuries, which represents approximately one half of one percent of the offences reported. Further, in 393 (91%) of the 433 cases the injury was listed as "minor."

To explore the nature of the violence in violent property crimes, all offence reports recorded by the police in Western Australia for 1992/93 where there was either a robbery (N=1,027) or a property crime accompanied by an offence against the person (N=435) were reviewed and classified. Each offence report contains a "narrative"—a description of the actual event in which the offence(s) occurred. This portion the report was used as the basis for the subsequent classification. The classification procedure aimed at isolating those cases most likely to contain instances of gratuitous violence for further investigation.

Forty (2.7%) of the cases had to be discarded as they were listed as false reports or had insufficient information. Most (69%) of the remaining offence reports involved forceful physical contact between the victim and offender. However, in only 55% of the cases involving a robbery offence alone was any physical contact made. In 148 of all the cases involving physical contact the context was a personal dispute (the victim and offender knew each other). Offence reports involving evidence of actual violence that was not part of a personal dispute were then examined to see if the violence was described in a way that could be classified as "instrumental" in either getting property or escaping from the crime scene. To meet this classification, the violence described needed to be relatively brief and directly related to the attempt by the offender to get the property or to escape. This operational definition of instrumental violence was applied to all the offence reports. Any cases involving considerable force that could not be readily ascertained as being related to getting the goods or getting away were grouped together for further investigation.

Eventually 25.9% (N=216) of cases of actual violence (with personal disputes excluded) fell into this category. Of the 216 cases where the violence was not classified as "instrumental," almost a quarter (N=52) appeared to involve a sexual motive. Because the classification procedure was designed to be over-inclusive, selecting into the final group all cases where there was doubt about the nature of the violence, many of the cases in the final category actually involved an instrumental motive even though this was not obvious from the narrative.

This analysis suggests that the intention of offenders engaged in most robberies and property crimes is to "get the goods and get away." Although victim resistance and other aspects of offender psychology that have been discussed may result in panic, confusion and ultimately violence, it does not appear that violence is intended by most offenders. Detailed interviews with victims and offenders are needed to explore more closely how offenders approach and deal with confrontations with victims in property crime situations. These will be described in the following sections.

OFFENDERS' PERSPECTIVES

Offenders' accounts were obtained from 88 prisoners held in Western Australian prisons in the latter part of 1993. Prisoners whose records indicated a conviction for a violent property crime were approached and invited to participate in the research. The selection procedure was not designed to achieve a sampling of any particular group such as armed robbers or those convicted of violent offences.

Prisoners were asked to read an "informed consent" form containing information about the research and stressing the voluntary nature of the prisoner's participation. It was explained that any violent property crime the offender had been engaged in could be the subject of the interview. The crime need not have led to conviction or even have been reported to the police. The only criteria were that the offenders themselves had to have used some force, and some theft had to have occurred. Perhaps because of the strict ethical requirements, such as signing the consent form, just over half (54%) of the offenders invited to participate in the research declined. The results should, therefore, be interpreted as suggestive, and caution should be adopted in generalising them to all violent property crime offenders.

Each prisoner could nominate one or two incidents of violence they personally had perpetrated in the course of a property crime. The majority (60%) could, or would, only nominate one incident for exploration. The 88 offenders interviewed reported a total of 123 incidents of violent property crime for analysis. Because the maximum number of incidents any one offender could offer was two, it is not likely that any particular offender or type of offender will significantly affect the range or type of incident discussed. Twenty-four (20%) of the incidents discussed involved a burglary; 42 (34%), a robbery in a shop; 27 (22%), a robbery in the street; 16 (13%), a car theft; and 14 (11%), disputes over drugs or other situations. The demography of the offenders interviewed closely resembled that of the state's prison population, 94% being male and 29% Aboriginal.

To check on the validity of offenders' accounts a number of prosecution files were reviewed. The review found that although some accounts "minimised" the extent of the violence used by offenders, or the offender chose to discuss offences of a less serious nature, there were also cases where offenders "maximised" their violence. That is, they talked about their violence as being more serious or extensive than revealed in the statement of facts compiled by the prosecution. As will be discussed further, it is important to view offenders' accounts critically, and to acknowledge that various distortions of memory and perception can combine to diminish the factual accuracy of their accounts.

Motive and Background to the Violence

The majority of motives (80%) given by offenders for their use of violence suggest that it was directly instrumental to the commission of the crime or the escape from the crime scene (in 9% it was sexual, and in the remaining 12% it involved interpersonal disputes, drug raids or other motives). Whether this accurately reflects offenders' motives, or simply the reality that offenders experience or are willing to project, is debatable. For example, in her study comparing 79 victim-offender pairs involved in violence, Morrison (1993) found that only 45% of the pairs agreed on the offenders' motivation for the attack.

Another problem with any attempt to reduce offenders' motives into one category is that searching for one motive for the use of violence fails to reflect the dynamic nature of these events. Although one motive may initially be present, the situation can shift quickly so that in the one scene there may be many motives operating.

"Instrumental" Motives

In almost half (49%) the cases analysed, offenders claimed violence was used to overcome the resistance of the victim, as illustrated in the following examples. Each account is labelled by the offender number (O.N.) to which it relates. In these cases the offenders considered that the violence used was necessary or justified.

> **O.N. 25**: *We counted the staff and then went in when we realised that all the staff had gone, except for the Manager. We went in, grabbed the Manager, threw him against the fridge door. He bounced off, I had a knife, the knife hit him. He thought that he was being attacked. He put his hands up. I thought he was going to attack me, so I stabbed him in the hand, then threw him on the ground.*

> **O.N. 94**: *I told the bloke to get on the floor, but he wouldn't listen. He was trying to cover up the cash box that was underneath the counter, and so he got down on his knees. He wouldn't lie face down on the floor with his hands behind his back. So I got him up, and I just hit him around the jaw and throat area. I got him down and once he was down, I just took the money away.*

These accounts suggest that from the offender's point of view the violence used is "instrumental," or "rationally" employed to achieve the goals of the crime. However, a threat of violence is usually sufficient to achieve the financial goals of the crime, and most robberies can be successfully carried out without the use of violence. Why then do offenders often use violence *before* demanding money, (for example, as in a mugging)? As discussed earlier, this type of robbery requires less skill and less courage. Offenders' accounts point to two other reasons why a mugging may be more attractive to an offender than a face-to-face robbery. First, victim compliance cannot be guaranteed, and the "violence first" approach overcomes any uncertainty. Second, unless the offender is equipped with a disguise, nonviolent confrontation gives the victim a chance to see the offender and thus identify him at a later stage. A mugging quickly disables the victim and minimises the opportunity for identification of the offender(s).

One implication of this line of reasoning is that where offenders perceive victim resistance to be likely, violence may initiate the robbery as a matter of course. A number of offenders suggested that "a good robbery is a quick robbery." Anything that could be done to minimise the time from initial contact to departure with the goods was desirable. From the offender's perspective, it was this time gap in which things could go wrong that was critical. A quick robbery maximises the robber's control through the advantage of surprise. The longer the encounter takes, the more chance there is that the victim can think about—or even mount—resistance, or that some other unexpected event may occur.

The issue of control does appear critical and it was a central construct in many robbers' accounts. A common fear expressed by robbers is that someone else will come along before the robbery is completed. The person who "comes along" is a threat because he or she is not already engaged in the scene, and the diversion of attention opens up new opportunities and possibilities for victims. Furthermore, the actions of the newcomer are likely to be more unpredictable. In one case, violence was used against one victim when another victim entered the scene. The violence was used to retain control of the victim whilst the other victim was dealt with:

O.N. 111

Interviewer: *What happened just before you hit him?*

Offender: *I just came up behind him, and I just sort of put the crow bar on his neck. Because it was cold, he must of thought it was a gun, and I said "listen, get down on the floor please, I don't want any trouble, face down." I had him on the ground. Then the lady comes out, and she walks in on us from this other room. She started screaming so I gave him a little whack, run over to her and grabbed her by the arm, and dragged her back over and said "get down on fucking ground, you bitch."*

Interviewer: *So you didn't hit him before he laid on the ground?*

Offender: *No.*

Interviewer: *And you hit him at that stage—why?*

Offender: *At the stage I had to hit him, because the lady came out from another office and starting screaming around. So I hit him and said "lay down" to him.*

Interviewer: *He was already laid down?*

Offender: *Yeh, I know, but I don't know why I say that—I had to say that to keep him laying down "don't get up," you know.*

The case cited above suggests that violence may sometimes be used for its strategic value. Although the use of violence was not "necessary," it worked to communicate the complete dominance of the offender and to reinforce the compliance of the victim. From the offender's viewpoint it was a case of "better to be safe than sorry."

Escape

In 30% of cases, offenders accounted for their use of violence as necessary to avoid capture and arrest. The "escape" motive may also be seen as instrumental, but in these situations violence is used not to perpetrate the crime but to escape from the crime scene. The thoughts of offenders in these cases concern the fear of being captured and/or physically beaten. In these examples, all the offenders saw the violence they used as necessary.

O.N. 13: *We were in a shop looking for the safe. Then we had security pull up. They checked the doors, and they realised we were in the building. Then they called the police. Then they came out of the car and kept walking up and down, and that yelling at us to come out and that. We ended up having to king hit them* [hit them hard] *with crow bars and that.*

O.N. 68: *I was involved in a break-in with another bloke, and I was in the house and the bloke came home. My co-offender took off and left me in there, and the bloke tried to hit me. So I ducked under his punch and put a screwdriver through his guts. I took off and his brother, or whoever it was that was there, followed me...*

Sexual

In 9% of cases of violence discussed, the nature of the violence was sexual. Sometimes the offender admitted to engaging in sexual assault when the opportunity became available, but claimed that the initial motivation was to complete a property crime. The alternative background is that the initial motive was sexual and the property crime occurred as an "add on." In some cases, the two motives are mixed, and it is difficult to determine the true sequence, if, indeed, there is one.

The link between the predatory nature of burglary and home-intrusion rape is illustrated in the following case. The offender explained that one night when he was very drunk he broke into a flat in the same block as where he was living. When he couldn't find any money he became frustrated (according to him) and raped the woman occupant. The offender responding to the question: "What thoughts were going through your head just before you raped her?" answered: "If I can't get any money I will have sex."

Other Motives

In the remaining 12% (N=15) of accounts the motives for violence varied, but most (N=9, 60% of this group) involved a motive that could be described as a vigilante action or some other form of retaliation, often in the context of drug deals. In a further three cases, the violence occurred in the context of an argument. In two cases the offender was unable to discern the main motive for the violence, and the remaining case was a paid contract bashing/robbery.

Offenders' Intoxication and Control over their Aggression

Although the picture emerging from offenders' accounts is dominated by instrumental considerations, offenders' use of drugs and alcohol is considerable, and this may affect their judgment and reactions. Seventy percent of offenders were intoxicated (with drugs and/or alcohol) or "hanging out" (experiencing withdrawal effects) when engaging in the violent property crime, as shown in Table 1. However, two-thirds of the offenders said they felt in control of their aggression. This apparent contradiction may be explained by the analysis provided by Cromwell et al. (1991). These authors suggest that burglars use drugs and alcohol to dampen their fear, thus allowing them to process more information on the crime scene, not less. It is argued that this is because the heightened state

of arousal associated with fear blocks the sort of "parallel processing"
needed by burglars to carry out the burglary and keep aware of danger at
the same time.

Table 1: Offenders' State and Type of Intoxication during Violent Property Crimes

Type of intoxication	Number	Percent
No drugs or alcohol	25	20.3
Alcohol but not "drunk"	12	9.8
"Hanging out" or "looping"	7	5.7
Alcohol—"drunk"	14	11.4
Cannabis alone	4	3.2
Alcohol and cannabis	13	10.6
Amphetamines alone	17	13.8
Amphetamines and other drugs	11	8.9
Heroin	7	5.7
Other drug combination	13	10.6
Total	123	100

Offenders' Perceptions on the Prevention of Violence in Property Crime

Offenders mostly described their emotions preceding the violence in terms of a justifiable anger or being placed in an "impossible position." During the actual violence, offenders reported that their thoughts were mainly concerned with "getting the job finished" (16%), overcoming victim resistance (18%) or avoiding capture (15%). In 10% of cases offenders could not recall clearly what they were thinking. In 16% of cases offenders stated categorically that they didn't think anything. In 8% of cases thoughts concerned "teaching the victim a lesson." In 5% of cases their thoughts focused on sex. In the remaining 11% of cases their thoughts varied over a range of foci. Much of the violence was described by offenders as spontaneous and reactive. Actions were commonly described as "instinctive" or determined directly by the actions of others. For example, confrontation by property owners was seen as leading to violence because it "was either him or me." A number of offenders argued that they "don't think" in the crime scene because everything happens too quickly.

A series of questions sought to explore how the violence the offender engaged in might have been avoided, and what might be done to prevent violence associated with property crime. In response to the question *"How do you think the victim could have handled the situation to have avoided the violence?,"* the most common reply was that "they couldn't," or the victim should simply not resist the demands of the offender or not try to capture or hinder the offender. These responses made up 84% of replies to this question.

On the subject of the prevention of violent property crime in general, it seemed as if most of the offenders were, again, quite fatalistic. The use of violence was described by many offenders as a natural part of life and accepted without revulsion. Comments that minimised the importance of violence and the effect of violence on victims were common. Many offenders talked about how they were brought up in environments where violence was common and thus "violence is just a part of life." Others explained the use of violence as necessary to deal with the challenges that faced them ("fight fire with fire"). The theme of desperation emerged in many offenders' accounts—that offenders are desperate and will do whatever is necessary to gain access to the property or avoid capture.

The question voiced by many in the community as to why car thieves should turn on the car owner rather than fleeing is addressed in a number of accounts. In this type of situation, two aspects of offenders' perceptions appear to be central. First, as discussed earlier, where an audience is present (particularly where the audience consists of fellow gang members), young offenders may seize the opportunity of physical advantage to display prowess.

Violence was explained by a number of offenders as defensive or precautionary. However, these perceptions need to be interpreted in the context of the cognitive distortions articulated by Novaco and Welsh (1989). Indeed, rather than seeing the victims' behaviour as justified, it appears that offenders often feel angry with the victim. In half the cases analysed, offenders reported feeling anger or excitement during the violence. The defiance of the victim is explained by the offender in the following account as an affront:

O.N. 21: *It made us angry that he thought he could stop us. He came up to us, but he could see there was a big mob of us.*

The appearance of the property owner may signal to an offender the need to fight, to get the property, to overcome the resistance of the victim or to defend himself against an expected attack. In the offender's state of intoxication, fear or anger, these motives may not be highly differentiated, as expressed in the following account:

O.N. 80:...*I* [had] *stolen a few cars, and people come running out and it looks like they want to use violence on you, so you just use it on them first.*

The message is that offenders engaged in a theft are in a highly volatile state, and, whether justified or not, they expect resistance and attempts by others to capture them. When confronted they may initiate violence (as they expect it from the owner) before thinking of running off, particularly if they judge their resources in the fight as superior.

The study of offenders' perspectives may help us understand why they perpetrate violence. However, offenders' accounts are likely to be flawed because memory is at least as subjective as perception, and it is likely that the material facts of the event in question are unlikely to be recalled with a high degree of accuracy. What may be remembered by the offender is not only likely to be a salutary interpretation of his or her actions but a distorted (and advantageous) remembrance of what actually happened. In other words, the cognitive distortions discussed earlier will not only lead to a misunderstanding in the offender of victim intention, but it will also contribute to a convenient—if unconscious—distortion of what actually happened in the event. One way to expose this memory distortion is through an examination of victims' accounts, particularly where these can be contrasted directly with the offender's accounts of the same incident. This is the purpose of the next section.

VICTIMS' PERSPECTIVES

To reach a group of victims of violent property crime, all offence reports containing a robbery offence or a combination of property and violent offences (N=1,462) for one year (1992/93) were reviewed. As explained earlier, in 216 cases there was actual violence, the event was not part of a dispute and the motive for the violence was not readily apparent (as being "instrumental" to the property crime or the offender's escape). Victims of these crimes may be able to explain something of the dynamics of violence in cases where the motive for the violence did not appear to be "instrumental" to the financial aspect of the crime.

The victims of these 216 incidents were approached by way of a letter posted by the police department. Victims were invited to post or phone back a reply to the request for an interview. Victims received in the envelope sent by the police two letters outlining the project, and another requesting that they contact the Crime Research Centre (a stamped, self-addressed envelope was included). Ten victims responded and were interviewed using a semi-structured questionnaire to probe their perceptions of what happened and how they responded. The selection procedure meant that the group contained an overrepresentation of victims of the most extreme forms of violence. Many of the victims of these more extreme forms of violence may have been reluctant to talk about their experience, or the low response rate may have been a product of the highly ethical but also highly cautious approach required in this research, which did not permit a more proactive strategy of inviting victim participation. Whatever the reason, the low response rate severely limits the generalizability of the findings, and this caution should be borne in mind when reading the following section.

Managing the Crime Scene

Almost all victims experienced feelings of shock, surprise, fear or horror when initially confronted by the offender. Thoughts during the situation mainly concerned survival. In most of the cases where the event took place for more than a few minutes, victims described how they began to think strategically about how to escape, avoid violence or get the offender out of the house. Most victims remained afraid that the offender(s) would use violence.

V.N. 1

Interviewer: *What was your intention when you were confronted by the offender(s)?*

Victim: *Survival. I did not want to give them any reason or justification for using violence.*

It seems trite to say that property is less valuable than physical integrity, yet some victims resist offenders and place themselves in great danger to "protect" their property. For example, when confronted by two young men who wanted his money, one elderly victim said "go ahead and try," which they subsequently did and beat him up badly. Rather than reassessing the value of his resistance, the victim was most upset at his inability to protect his own property and intimated that he had taken action to increase his ability to defend himself in the future. However, most victims appear to quickly calculate their points of vulnerability and strength, as do offenders. For example, for women alone in a house having children present adds to their vulnerability and they are likely to comply with the offender's demands in an effort to protect their children.

Victims' Perception of Offenders' Motives for the Violence

Victims' perceptions of offenders' motives varied, but there were some interesting points of contrast. A number of victims mentioned how offenders seemed to be enjoying the violence. Only one of the 88 offenders interviewed admitted enjoying violence, and in none of the offenders' accounts was mention made of any laughter associated with violence. But this association (laughter as the violence was perpetrated) did emerge in three of the ten victim accounts. The data set, however, is not representative as it was specifically designed to exclude the majority of encounters where the violence used appeared to be minor and limited to the instrumental function of getting the goods or getting away. The following examples illustrate how victims saw the sense of power enjoyed by the offender as being a substantial motivator for the violence:

V.N. 9

Interviewer: *What do you think the motive of the offender was when he entered the scene?*

Victim: *To break into the service station.*

Interviewer: *Do you think they actually enjoyed the violence?*

Victim: *Oh, yes, they enjoyed the violence. No two ways about it—he knew he had the* **power**... *He was psyched up to do it. He was liking the power.*

V.N. 7

Interviewer: *What do you think the motive of the offender was when he entered the scene?*

Victim: *Strictly getting a thrill—he was not deterred by my husband at all.*

V.N. 2

Interviewer: *Why did they keep kicking you after they got the wallet?*

Victim: *Because they've got the upper hand—one starts to weaken, the [offender] got pleasure, he was laughing...he loved it.*

Lyng (1993) has suggested that young males may be attracted into crime because it presents an opportunity to confront their fear, and the overcoming of fear is particularly exhilarating for young men (see also Daly and Wilson, 1994, on the young male syndrome). The contrasting perceptions of victims and offenders on issues of how offenders appear whilst perpetrating violence is a potentially productive form of further research, and may be a useful source for therapeutic intervention with violent offenders.

Contrasting Victims' Accounts with Offenders' Accounts

The difference between the accounts of victims and offenders is most dramatically demonstrated when both describe the same incident. Only two such comparison cases are available in the present study. In one of the most graphic incidents of violent property crime, the victim described how the offender perpetrated various acts of violence for over three hours. The offender, however, gave a different story:

> **O.N. 3**: ...*When they said they would call the police, I said I wouldn't be there when the police arrived. I turned to leave, they stood in the doorway and said... "you're not leaving till the police arrive." ...I tried to push him out of the way, he grabbed hold of my shirt, and I gave him a punch. And then I felt a pain in my back...* [the offender then describes how he ran out of the house away from the victims].

The victim of this offender described a totally different scene, which he and the other victims were set upon by the offender. According to the victim, the offender proceeded to brutally bash and terrorise, them after which, in fear of his life, he made a feeble (the victim was elderly and the offender young) attempt to retaliate:

Victim's account of the same situation:

The victim is describing the offender's first act of violence, which followed the offender being confronted directly by a co-victim, "Jack":

> **V.N. 6**: ...*He then switched completely. First he screamed, then took his arm back and hit Jack in the face.*
>
> *He was standing in front of the door and made no effort to go. Blood splattered in all directions, He gave blows to each person. He went berserk, he was totally in control. He made no attempt to escape. He then turned around and ordered Jack and Bill into the kitchen. He looked around for me and said "you too." He terrorised us for three hours.*

These two cases, where the victim and offender accounts are available from the same situation, illustrate how important it is to compare the two perspectives. Other accounts from victims contained on prosecution files also often contradict the accounts given by offenders. The point is important because it is quite possible that these contrasting accounts represent more than the convenient reconstruction of events by the offender. It is possible that victims and offenders view the same event very differently, and it is particularly where these views most differ that the chances for violence are maximised. After the event, both victim and offender may be motivated to remember the situation in a way that rationalises their own behaviour.

In the case where the young offender beat three elderly men, and in the earlier situation where an elderly man confronted two young offenders, the victims had underestimated their vulnerability and may have assumed that the age status would be sufficient to claim dominance. However, at least in the case involving three victims, the offender probably did feel as if he was about to be apprehended. The violence may, therefore, have begun as part of an escape attempt, though it appears to quickly have become much more than that.

The contrasting perspectives of victims and offenders can be used to illustrate the importance of victim precautionary measures. This subject is explored further in the following section.

INTEGRATING VICTIM AND OFFENDER PERSPECTIVES INTO CRIME PREVENTION

Criminological approaches to crime prevention typically focus on offenders: offender motivation, offender decision making and offender rehabilitation. However, everyday efforts at crime prevention are largely initiated by victims or potential victims. Victim behaviour, including victim demeanour, is critical in minimising the likelihood of both personal and property crime. Many women reduce the likelihood of predatory victimisation by restricting their activity cycles, and people in general avoid confrontations that may become violent. The social and personal consequences of these forms of crime prevention are not usually considered in criminology. Recently, Felson and Clarke (1995) have discussed the notion of integrating a study of routine precautions taken by citizens into the study of crime prevention. Such an integration could incorporate the routine avoidance of potentially violent situations.

There are a number of ways to think about efforts at preventing violence in the course of a robbery or a property crime, which I have described in more detail elsewhere (see Indermaur, 1995). In relation to the role of the victim in crime prevention, it is possible to conceptualise two levels. First, and probably most important, the potential victim prevents crime through routine precautions and activities that minimise the likelihood of coming into contact with offenders and/or violence. The range of activities that citizens engage in to avoid violence is profound. Strategies, sometimes conscious and sometimes unconscious, range from choosing to live in a safe suburb to avoiding walking on certain streets (or streets anywhere). Crime prevention is integrated into many everyday practices and Felson and Clarke (in press) point out that individuals devote considerable attention to avoiding crime through taking routine precautions. The curtailment of routine activity associated with the fear of crime is a large subject worthy of greater study. Certain sectors of the population, such as women and the elderly, take greater precautions because they believe, rightly or wrongly, that they are at risk and that victimisation will have extensive and permanent effects on their quality of life.

The second level at which a potential victim minimises violence is once the confrontation with the offender has begun. This area of influence can be described as "crime scene management," and relates to the literature on victim resistance. In a situation in which the victim is confronted by an offender, he or she may be able to avoid or minimise violence by complying with the offender's demands and not attempting to restrain the offender. Especially where the offender is engaged in stealing property, the facilitation of the offender's essential mission (to get the goods and get away) would seem the safest course of action. However, many victims choose to try and protect their property (women clutch their handbags and men rush out of the house to confront car thieves), and would object to an attitude of "giving in" to criminals.

The issue of resistance may also interact with the psychological needs of the victim. It may be important to some victims to resist even if they are not likely to be successful. For example, one victim of a vicious attack objected to the standard "don't resist" advice. This victim argued that it was important to a victim's self-esteem not to just give in to an attack but to fight back. The victim, who had suffered severe injuries, also focused on both the psychological and larger social consequences of a policy of non-resistance. However, as noted earlier, the relationship between resistance and injury is complex. And, as pointed out by Cook (1987), non-resistance is no guarantee of non-injury and, in some cases, victims will minimise injury through their resistance.

Understanding where the offender is "coming from" may help victims consider their options. Property offenders are generally highly excited and afraid of intervention by victims or guardians. In this context anything that "raises the alarm" and invites intervention, such as a scream, will be threatening to the offender and may work to precipitate an escape. However, the risk with this strategy is that the offender, either through panic or in a calculated way, may attack the victim to eliminate the noise. Although some robbers may expect and plan for the sounding of an alarm, a more effective strategy for burglars and car thieves may be to bring the offender's attention to the likelihood of an alarm being sounded. This is the principle behind the display of car alarm warnings, lights and decals.

The general principle underlying all these strategies is to make it more attractive to the offender to avoid confrontation or to flee the scene as quickly as possible. From the offender's point of view, the unknown factors are the size and nature of a victim's resources and how quickly support will arrive. Victims would be well advised to maximise the chances that offenders will perceive that they have been (or will be) detected. In this regard, it is interesting to note how the proliferation of portable phones and video surveillance cameras will add to the possibilities for victims to raise the alarm. To be most effective, these possibilities should be drawn to the attention of offenders or potential offenders. Portable phones (with memory dialing) should perhaps be made available to people in vulnerable service industries and in locations where crime is more likely to occur. Advertising the fact that alarms can be raised instantaneously could make a target much less attractive to some thieves, although others may include the likelihood of an alarm sounding in their planning and still judge that the rewards outweigh the risks.

As the statistics on robbery violence suggest, most offenders want to complete a property crime without interference or violence. Apart from robbers, most offenders do not seek, or welcome, a confrontation with a victim. Partly because of the anxiety of being discovered and partly because of drug and/or alcohol intoxication, offenders may not operate rationally or be easy to reason with when confronted. A combination of strategic planning to avoid opportunities for robbery, together with a better appreciation of the ways victims can, and do, prevent crime and the escalation of crime, appears to offer the most hope in reducing the already low rate of injury associated with robbery and property crime. In general, the safest course of action to reduce victim injury in regard to property offenders appears to be to encourage and facilitate the escape of the offender. Recent moves in Australia that seek to arm the potential victim are more likely to result in encouraging victims to confront offenders, leading to preventable injuries in both victims and offenders.

REFERENCES

Australian Bureau of Statistics (1994). *Crime and Safety Australia, April 1993*. Catalogue No. 4509.0. Canberra, AUS: Commonwealth Government Printer.

Cook, P.J. (1985). "Is Robbery Becoming More Violent? An Analysis of Robbery Murder Trends since 1968." *Journal of Criminal Law and Criminology* 76:480-489.

—— (1986). "The Relationship between Victim Resistance and Injury in Non Commercial Robbery." *Journal of Legal Studies* 1:405-416.

—— (1987). "Robbery Violence." *Journal of Criminal Law and Criminology* 78:357-376.

Cromwell, P.F., J.N. Olson and D.W. Avary (1991). *Breaking and Entering: An Ethnographic Analysis of Burglary*. Newbury Park, CA: Sage.

Daly, M. and M. Wilson (1994). "Evolutionary Psychology of Male Violence." In: J. Archer (ed.), *Male Violence*. London, UK: Routledge.

Dodge, K.A., J.M. Price, J. Bachorowski and J.P. Newman (1990). "Hostile Attributional Biases in Severely Aggressive Adolescents." *Journal of Abnormal Psychology* 99:385-392.

Driscoll, J. (1982). "Perception of Aggressive Interaction as a Function of the Perceiver's Aggression." *Perceptual and Motor Skills* 54:1123-1134.

Felson, M. and R.V. Clarke (1995). "Routine Precautions, Criminology and Crime Prevention." In: H. Barlow, (ed.), *Crime and Public Policy: Putting Theory to Work*. Boulder, CO: Westview Press.

Gabor, T., M. Baril, M. Cusson, D. Elie, M. LeBlanc, and A. Normandeau (1987). *Armed Robbery: Cops, Robbers and Victims*. Springfield, IL: Charles C Thomas.

Grace, S. (1993). "Resisting Sexual Assault: A Review of the Literature." *Home Office Research Bulletin* 34:18-25.

Harding, R.W. and A. Blake (1989). *Weapon Choice by Violent Offenders in Western Australia: A Pilot Study*. Research report No. 1. Nedlands, WA: Crime Research Centre, University of Western Australia.

Indermaur, D. (1995). *Violent Property Crime*. Sydney, AUS: Federation Press.

Katz, J. (1988). *Seductions of Crime: Moral and Sensual Attractions of Doing Evil*. New York, NY: Basic Books.

Lyng, S. (1993). "Dysfunctional Risk Taking: Criminal Behaviour as Edgework." In: N.J. Bell and R.W. Bell (eds.), *Adolescent Risk Taking*. Newbury Park, CA: Sage.

Morrison, S. (1993). "Both Sides of the Story: A Comparison of the Perspectives of Offenders and Victims Involved in a Violent Incident." *Home Office Research Bulletin* 34:26-30.

New South Wales Bureau of Crime Statistics and Research (1987). *An Analysis of Robbery in New South Wales*. Sydney, AUS: Attorney General's Department.

Novaco, R.W. and W.N. Welsh, (1989). "Anger Disturbances: Cognitive Mediation and Clinical Prescriptions." In: K. Howells and C. Hollin (eds.), *Clinical Approaches to Violence*. Chichester, UK: Wiley.

Shelly, E.L. and H.H. Toch (1968). "The Perception of Violence as an Indicator of Adjustment in the Institutionalised Offender." In: H. Toch and H.C. Smith (eds.), *Social Perception: The Development of Interpersonal Impressions. An Enduring Problem in Psychology*. Princeton, NJ: Van Nostrand.

Short, R.J., and R.J. Simeonsson (1986). "Social Cognition and Aggression in Delinquent Adolescent Males." *Adolescence* 21:159-176.

Warr, M. (1988). "Rape, Burglary and Opportunity." *Journal of Quantitative Criminology* 4:275-288.

Wolfgang, M. and F. Ferracuti (1967). *The Subculture of Violence: Towards an Integrated Theory in Criminology*. London, UK: Tavistock.

AN ANALYSIS OF THE DECISION-MAKING PRACTICES OF ARMED ROBBERS

by

Shona A. Morrison

Commonwealth Law Enforcement Board,

Canberra, AUS

and

Ian O'Donnell

University of Oxford

and Linacre College

Abstract: This paper is based on a study of commercial armed robbery in London, UK, involving the analysis of over 1,000 police reports and inter- views with 88 incarcerated armed robbers. While official criminal statistics document that over three-quarters of armed robberies in Britain involve real firearms, findings suggested that only around one-third actually do. Robbers rarely reported the availability of guns to be an important factor in their choice of weapon. Together, this implies that simply reducing the availability of real firearms may not be the most effective preventive strategy. Offenders made reasonably accurate predictions with regard to the financial benefits of the crime. Also, their analyses of the potential costs involved in committing armed robbery were found to be neither irrational nor grounded in ignorance of the likely outcome. Furthermore, robbers appeared to tailor their modus operandi with a view to both maximizing the potential financial rewards and reducing the likely risks involved in the crime. Target hardening and other situational

Address correspondence to: Shona Morrison, Office of Strategic Crime Assessments, Locked Bag 23, Queen Victoria Terrace, Canberra, ACT 2600, Australia.

crime prevention strategies have uses beyond their primary prevention capabilities. For instance, they may aid in the subsequent detection of offenders. This, in addition to further study on the dynamics of robbers' motivations, may lead to an effective broad based approach to the prevention of commercial armed robbery.

INTRODUCTION

Armed robbery can cause physical injury or even death, fear in the community, emotional trauma and, of course, financial loss. Thus, one of the main priorities for researchers who investigate this activity is to provide knowledge that may help in the advance of effective crime prevention strategies. Although commercial armed robbery has received some research attention over the years, progress in preventing this crime has been slow, as evidenced by an escalation in rates of armed robbery around the world. Seemingly, every technological or strategic advance made in the preventive arsenal is matched by sophistication (in a small number of cases) or sheer determination (in a much larger number of cases) on the parts of robbers.

Related to this is the problem that armed robbery is not a specialist crime (Gabor et al., 1987). Generally, it does not require great physical strength (the presence of a weapon replaces this need), intellectual power, technical know-how or even "street wisdom," such as contacts with "middle men." Thus, other than in the most sophisticated robberies, the effort involved would appear to be little while the payout is (relatively speaking) large.

The Robber as Decision Maker

That the actual behavior involved in armed robbery is, in most cases, uncomplicated is not in dispute. However, it is not necessarily the case that the cognitive, social and psychological processes underlying these crimes are equally elementary. For instance, robbers must first decide whether they are prepared to attempt to obtain goods—or, more commonly, money—illegally. They then have to consider robbery to be an "acceptable" and achievable crime. The sorts of learning processes that are necessary for this decision to be reached are not examined here. This should not suggest that these processes are unimportant; on the contrary, they are crucial to our understanding of robbery. The circumstances and decisions immediately surrounding the robbery _event_, however, are equally significant. Furthermore, an understanding of event-related issues may assist in the development and evaluation of practical preventive measures.

Once the resolution has been made to commit a robbery, a number of important decisions follow, such as how much money is "required" and what kind of target would have to be attacked in order to realize the financial expectations. Crucial factors at this juncture would be the offender's opinions about the kind of weaponry required for the offense— whether a real, replica or "simulated" firearm would be most appropriate— and his preparedness to fire a gun should his threats need to be reinforced at any stage during the robbery. Depending on the target, his ability to organize others to cooperate in such a risky venture may also be significant. These choices would be influenced, in turn, by the offender's access to firearms, his previous experience of armed robbery and his psychological makeup.

The modus operandi may embody a simple structure such as a lone robber with an imitation pistol who walks into a petrol station late at night and demands cash before escaping on foot. Or it may be a more complex scheme involving several robbers, "scanners" to listen into police radio waves, an array of lethal weaponry and two or more getaway cars, with a cash-in-transit van as the target. Whether relatively straightforward or organized and sophisticated, these schemes and the decisions underlying them may provide important indicators of potential preventive techniques (e.g., Feeney, 1986; Harding and Blake, 1989; Kapardis, 1988).

The study of criminal decision making evolved from the rational choice, or economic model of crime (for concise reviews, see Akers [1990], Cornish and Clarke [1986], and Walters [1994]). This perspective, and the preventive strategies that follow from it, is founded on the assumption that offenders are more or less rational in their decision making and seek to benefit themselves by their criminal activity (Gabor et al., 1987). Thus, a better understanding of the cognitive transactions behind their plans of action, and the potential costs and benefits of committing a particular offence, may lead to the cultivation of useful crime prevention strategies. As this approach is based upon a model of the offender as responding to net incentives, it is hypothesized that if the cost-benefit ratio associated with a particular action is changed so that the likely benefits are outweighed by the likely costs, then the potential offenders' choices will change accordingly and fewer such crimes will be committed. If the model of the rational offender is not valid, this has important implications for general deterrence. A useful discussion of the theoretical perspective on the deterrence process is contained in Cook (1980).

It is, however, difficult to assess either the extent to which offenders behave rationally, or the circumstances under which an appropriate *modus operandi* is devised, without interviewing them. Such inquiries would focus on how they modify their behavior to take account of their perceptions of the opportunities afforded by different physical environments, and their subjective evaluations of different schedules of reward and punishment.

Some researchers have typified the robber as a carefully calculating rational actor. In Western Australia, for instance, Harding and Blake (1989) interviewed violent offenders, including a number of armed robbers, whom they portrayed as careful decision makers. They found that robbers who had used firearms put some effort into planning their crime and were likely to have investigated in advance the security arrangements of their chosen target. These offenders also claimed to have given some thought to the possibility of being caught and the likely sentence if convicted. Indeed, these researchers portrayed the gun robber as a "top-of-the-range" criminal.

However, other research sheds a different light upon the perpetrators of armed robbery. From the 100 armed robbers he interviewed in Melbourne, AUS, Kapardis (1988) learned that almost two-thirds of the robberies that they committed were carried out within 24 hours of the idea being conceived, with just under one-half being committed within six hours. Almost half had been drinking alcohol prior to the commission of the offence. Similarly, Haran and Martin (1984) found that the majority of the 500 American bank robbers in their sample did little pre-planning.

Feeney (1986) also reported that most of his sample of 113 California robbers, just over half of whom used guns, took a highly casual approach to their crimes. Most claimed to have done no planning at all, and only one in 20 planned in any detail. Generally, the amount of planning increased with the number of robberies committed, although over 60% of the offenders said that they had not even thought about getting caught before they carried out the robbery. Gabor et al. (1987) interviewed 39 convicted armed robbers in Montreal. They discovered that no disguises were worn in three-quarters of the incidents studied, the typical amount of money stolen was modest, and the most frequent mode of escape was on foot.

Very little research relating to armed crime has been produced by British researchers, with the notable exception of Greenwood (1972), McClintock and Gibson (1961), and Weatherhead and Robinson (1970). Nonetheless, even this work devoted little space to the analysis of robbery. This is understandable, however, because at the time this work was carried out armed robbery was not a significant problem.

Preventing Armed Robbery

Application of the economic model of, or decision-making approach to, armed robbery has led to the development of a number of mainly situational crime prevention strategies. A comprehensive discussion of crime prevention is beyond the scope of this paper, but for recent debate, refer to Pease (1994), and Sutton (1994), and for a good overview of successful preventive techniques, see Clarke (1992). The development of target-hardening devices, training regimes to inform employees of the best course of action in the event of a robbery, and sophisticated surveillance equipment make up an impressive defensive arsenal. Of course, some caution must always be exercised in evaluating the merits, or potential merits, of crime prevention strategies. It has been documented, for instance, that these strategies may incur unintended consequences (see Grabosky chapter in this volume), the most omnipresent of which is "displacement" (e.g., Barr and Pease, 1990). In other words, preventive strategies that appear to have been successful in preventing one crime may simply have led to the perpetration of another one elsewhere, with the result that there is no overall beneficial effect. The different forms that displacement may take have been described by Reppetto (1976) and by Clarke (1983). Pease (1994) presents a more optimistic view of this phenomenon.

Other unintended consequences may stem from the robber's response to the deterrent hardware put in place by his chosen target. For instance, in an attempt to prevent the activation of "pop-up" screens or alarms, hostage taking may be employed. Also, surveillance equipment may increase the robber's use of disguises, thereby increasing the level of intimidation and decreasing victims' subsequent powers of identification. Furthermore, knowledge of practices designed to protect employees, such as advising them to hand over cash without objection (Health and Safety

Executive, 1993), may have served to convince a number of otherwise reticent robbers that it is an easy crime or a "safe bet." Thus, it is not surprising to find that suggestions for robbery prevention often attract considerable criticism (Barr and Pease, 1990).

It may be indicative of the difficulties inherent in promoting straight-forward strategies for crime prevention that what efforts have been made have been made largely at reducing the robber's access to his most favored weapon, the firearm. Evidence for this may be found in the vast quantity of literature devoted to discussion about the link between guns and crime. In general, it is believed that should firearms be made less accessible to potential lawbreakers, then all armed crime, including armed robbery, would be dramatically reduced (e.g., Cook, 1983; Gabor et al., 1987; Greenwood, 1972; Wright et al., 1983; Zimring and Hawkins, 1973). The assumption that the availability of firearms is the crux of robbery prevention deserves further attention.

The "Firearms Debate"

A substantial proportion of the publications about firearms and crime focus on the issue of firearms availability and legislation—commonly referred to as the "firearms debate." The U.S. captures the most attention because of its particular problem of violence, use of firearms and wide-spread availability of lethal weapons (e.g., Berry, 1991; Cook, 1983). While an intense discussion of the various arguments proposed on either side of the firearms debate is beyond the scope of this paper (but see Cook, 1983 and Kleck, 1991), the principal thrust of debate deserves some analysis. Leaving aside the issue of replica weapons use for the moment, the proposition that widespread availability of firearms profoundly influences levels of armed crime entails two quite distinct questions. First, what is the relationship between the availability of *legitimate* firearms and armed crime? Second, what is the relationship between the *illegal* firearms market and armed crime?

The relationship between firearms legislation and the use of legally held guns is an exceptionally complicated one. Overall, there is little conclusive evidence to show that the availability of *legitimate* firearms directly influences their use in crime, or that more restrictive firearms legislation helps to reduce the number of guns falling into the wrong hands (Berry, 1991; Maybanks, 1992; Newton and Zimring, 1969; Polsby, 1994; Robin,

1993; Wright and Rossi, 1986; Wright et al., 1986). Instead, there would appear to be a stronger suggestion that an abundance of *illegal* firearms (an unknown proportion of which will once have been legally held) has helped feed the increasing levels of armed crime in Britain today. However, this assumption begs four fundamental questions. First, is there in fact a large and growing black market in illegal weapons (official statistics fail to accurately identify how many armed robberies actually involve real firearms rather than imitation or simulated guns)? Second, are criminals aware of this illegal pool? Third, do they have the means to access it? And fourth, are criminals *prepared* to use firearms in the execution of their crimes? The link between the availability of illegal firearms and crime appears more tenuous when viewed in this way (Harding, 1993).

Background to the Research

The U.K. Home Office Research and Planning Unit, at the request of F8 Division of the Metropolitan Police Department, commissioned the present research to examine the increasing use of firearms in robbery, together with the apparently widespread and easy availability of guns to those who wish to use them for criminal purposes and the dearth of information about the circumstances in which armed robberies take place. Particular emphasis was placed on the decisions made by robbers.

The research evolved from the analytical realm of rational choice theories of crime. The rational choice models developed by criminologists have not been based upon the assumption that offenders take account of all relevant factors on every occasion when an offence is contemplated (Clarke, 1983). Rather than assuming perfect utility maximization, they have tended to work with the concept of "bounded," or "limited," rationality (Simon, 1955). Thus, a number of factors that are unrelated to the decision to commit an offence can influence an offender's behavior. Such factors may include alcohol intoxication or the desire to stave off the unpleasant withdrawal symptoms associated with certain drug addictions. According to Akers (1990), rationality may also be limited by lack of information (for example, not having an accurate appreciation of the probability of arrest, or underestimating the likely sentence), by values and by other "non-rational" influences.

While examining the factors that robbers *did* take into account in their decision making, it is equally interesting to note the factors that they *failed* to accommodate. Discounted factors are, after all, as much a component of rational decision making as are positive factors (Harding, 1993). Furthermore, deterrence is based on the assumption that the costs of committing a crime will be weighed with as much zeal as the benefits to be gained. So, it is important to determine whether present attempts at crime prevention are being appreciated by those they are aimed at (and if so, why, in the case of these convicted robbers at least, they have clearly failed to have the desired deterrent effect). Walsh's (1986) discovery of "free-range negative thinking" is interesting in that it suggests that economic criminals do assess the reasons for *not* committing an offence. However, the bulk of the analysis reported by Walsh appears to rest on the practical considerations of the crime rather than on the decision to commit a crime.

The study reported here examined an abundance of factors that may or may not have influenced the robber's decisions for instance, weapon choice and weapon availability, preparedness to employ violence, acquaintance with potential accomplices, perceptions of the degree of difficulty involved in robbing different targets, and, of course, the motivations behind the crime. Perhaps more importantly, the study also explored the interactions among different factors.

This paper summarizes some of these results in the context of two main foci. First, the priority given to the firearms debate and the topic of availability of firearms is critically examined in the light of evidence of rates of firearms use. Using existing sources of data, it is not possible to estimate the frequency with which the firearms described by witnesses were real or imitation, loaded or unloaded. One of the main aims of this study was to investigate the frequency with which guns used in robbery were capable of discharging lethal shots and to find out what factors motivated robbers to choose different types of weapons. Second, the study examined those factors that are relevant to the immediate calculation of whether to commit robbery. How does the robber's assessment of the benefits to be gained from committing the crime (i.e., the financial gain) compare with the costs associated with the crime (such as the risk of arrest, the risk of facing a long prison term and the risk of being shot by police—a risk that, for the British robber, is a relatively new consideration). Factors relating to the decision to commit robbery have received very little research attention, despite the fact that primary preventive efforts are likely to impact most upon this equation.

METHOD

The focus of the study was commercial armed robbery, as opposed to personal or "street" robbery. Initially, information was drawn from police records of all armed robberies and attempted robberies dealt with by the Central Robbery Squad, the specialist robbery team, of the Metropolitan Police in the London area during 1990. All incidents of robbery (including attempts) that take place in the Metropolitan Police District (MPD) and are known, or believed, to have involved a firearm or imitation firearm are subject to special recording procedures. When such offences are reported to the police, a document called a "specrim" (a report of a *specially interesting crime*), that gives a brief outline of where and when the offence took place and the details of any suspects, should be sent within 24 hours from the police division where the offence occurred to the General Registry. This registry is the Metropolitan Police repository for files concerning serious crimes. If the incident involved an attack on a security company, bank, building society, post office, betting shop or jewelry store, then a specrim should also be sent to the Central Robbery Squad (commonly known as the "Flying Squad") at New Scotland Yard.

Using the registry files relating to every recorded armed robbery in 1990, we noted: (1) the date, time, and place where the offence occurred; (2) the type of target attacked and the amount of money and other property stolen; (3) how the offence was brought to the attention of the police and the nature of the police response; (4) whether any injuries were reported and the circumstances under which they were sustained; and (5) the modus operandi of the robbers, including the number of offenders, their gender and ethnic group, whether disguises were worn, the number and type of guns and other weapons employed, how demands were made, if the offence involved a team, the roles played by different team members, the context in which firearms were discharged, and anything known about the provenance of a recovered firearm. Details about the offender were accessed through the National Identification Bureau using each offender's criminal record number. From these files we learned the name, date of birth, occupation, employment status, educational achievements, and marital status of anyone convicted of the offence, along with the dates of all previous court appearances, the nature of the charges brought and the sentences received, and the details of the present robbery charge and sentence.

The purpose of this initial data collection was to provide a cross-sectional picture, or snapshot, of the characteristics and circumstances of the phenomenon of recorded armed robbery as experienced during a single calendar year in London—the police area in Britain where the greatest number of robberies with firearms has traditionally been recorded. Because of its reliance upon data derived from files deposited with the General Registry, most of which had been dealt with by the Central Robbery Squad, the study is undoubtedly biased toward those offences considered by police to be the more serious. In total, data were collected for 1,134 incidents of robbery where a firearm, or what appeared to be a firearm, had been produced by the offender, or where the offender had given the impression through his actions and the contents of written or verbal demands that he possessed a gun, even though one had not actually been seen by witnesses.

With regard to the decisions and calculations of armed robbers, the most valuable information was gleaned directly from the perpetrators of these crimes themselves. Thus, a substantial part of this 18-month study was dedicated to interviewing convicted armed robbers in prison about the decisions they made regarding their crimes and, more importantly, their explanations and evaluations of those decisions.

The analysis of police records yielded 146 potential interviewees who had all, so far as we could tell, been involved in discrete robberies. To avoid the collection of duplicate information in relation to robberies involving "teams," we only approached one member of each "robbery unit" who was still in custody when the fieldwork was being carried out. However, a further 46 of these individuals (including the only female robber in the sample) had been discharged from prison by the time we tried to make contact with them, could not be traced at the prison in which we were told he was located, were unavailable due to medical or administrative reasons or, in two cases, had absconded. Thus, we managed to speak to 100 prisoners, although nine of these interviews were later discarded and five individuals refused to be interviewed. However, in two of these cases it was possible to substitute an alternative team member who consented to be interviewed, resulting in a final sample of 88 completed interviews.

The final interview sample constituted 41% of the total sample of robbers (N=214) recorded as having been convicted of armed robberies in 1990 and for whom records were available. It thus became important to examine the representativeness of the interview sample by comparing the characteristics of this group to the complete sample of convicted robbers.

We found that the two samples varied very little with regard to gender, ethnicity, place of birth, age at which full-time education had been completed and formal educational qualifications. Nor were there any significant differences between the general and interview samples in relation to age at the time of the robbery, employment status, marital status and previous experience with the criminal justice system. Therefore, the robbers we interviewed appeared representative of all known armed robbers with respect to a variety of important sociodemographic and criminological features. Also, when the details of the offences for which the interviewed robbers had been convicted were compared with the overall pattern of incidents of serious armed robberies contained in the total sample of recorded incidents, it appeared that the offences discussed with the interviewed robbers were broadly representative of all those carried out in the MPD in 1990. However, it seems reasonable to postulate that this group of robbers, all of whom were still serving prison sentences some three years after the commission of the crime, contained those who had been involved in the most serious armed robberies.

The interviews, involving one interviewer and one inmate, took place out of the sight and hearing of prison staff. The aims of the study were explained in detail, and prospective participants were assured of total confidentiality. They were told that if there were any questions they did not wish to answer they should simply say so, and that particular line of inquiry would be pursued no further. They were offered no inducements to participate. This strategy proved extremely successful in that 95% of those inmates who were approached in person agreed to be interviewed.

The in-depth, semi-structured interviews were designed to elicit descriptions of the offender's decision making throughout the planning and commission of the robbery. Interviews, of course, do have some general drawbacks. In particular, it is difficult to estimate how closely self-reported data accurately reflect actual "on-the-spot" cognitions, perceptions, decisions or even behavior. This can occur because the interviewee: actively attempts to mislead the interviewer by providing inaccurate details; fails to report aspects of the incident that he has simply forgotten; or inadvertently provides a description of the incident that has been contaminated over time by post hoc rationalizations and justifications.

The potential for inaccuracy generated by the first two problems—misleading the interviewer and forgetting details of the incident—can be substantially reduced by careful wording and validating interview data, wherever possible, against information collected from other sources (Cannell and Kahn, 1968; Hessing and Elffers, 1995). For instance, we were able to compare the information obtained from offenders regarding the type of target attacked, the number of accomplices, the amount of money stolen, and previous criminal histories, with the information that had already been collected from police files. A high degree of concordance emerged. Also, the likelihood of being intentionally misled was reduced due to the emphasis placed on the interviewee's privilege to refuse to answer any questions with which he felt uncomfortable.

The third potential source of inaccuracy in self-reported data—being provided with rationalized versions of an event rather than data that truly reflects the offender's perceptions and attitudes at the time—is more difficult to overcome. The tendency of human beings to retrieve information from memory that has been unconsciously altered has been well-documented in textbooks on cognitive psychology, in articles on courtroom testimony, and, more recently, in several sociological, psychological, and criminological studies that have involved the use of interviews as the main research tool (e.g., Abelson and Levi, 1985; Berger and Luckmann, 1971; Cannell and Kahn, 1968; Gabor et al., 1987; Indermaur, 1994; Scott and Lyman, 1968; Sykes and Matza, 1957). On the whole, researchers acknowledge this limitation of the interview as a research method but still regard it as a valuable and sometimes indispensable method of obtaining retrospective information. Moreover, depending upon the purpose of the study, the problem of hindsight rationalization may not be as serious as it first appears. To examine this proposition, it is important to understand something about the way in which human information processing and decision making operates.

First, the study of heuristics in cognitive psychology has revealed that short cuts, including some degree of rationalization, are present *at the time* when decisions are made (Abelson and Levi, 1985; Priest and McGrath, 1970). Distortion may play a role in convincing not only others but the individuals themselves that their behavior is justified (Agnew, 1990). Thus, descriptions of the way in which decisions were reached may be more accurate reflections of the cognitive processes at the time than researchers generally suppose. Related to this is the fact that decisions are regularly based on what has been termed "standing" decisions, or "templates." In other words, the mental labor involved in formulating the answer to the decision problems are carried out the first time the situation is encountered. Thereafter, rules or standing decisions exist that govern and greatly simplify subsequent dilemmas of a similar nature. For instance, the smoker does not go through the process of deciding whether or not to smoke cigarettes each time he or she goes to light one up. In reality, the decision to smoke has been made and each cigarette is smoked on the basis of this predetermined conclusion. Similarly, the robber, unless it is the first time he or she has considered this crime, is likely to be acting in a manner that invokes little contemplation, as the resolution to obtain money in this way has already been made. Of course, it is of interest also to understand why individuals choose to commit robbery in the first place, but it is equally important to appreciate the processes and justifications that allow them to persist in committing this crime.

Second, psychological studies of information retrieval have refuted the proposition that individuals cannot provide reasonably accurate, retrospective protocols to describe their thought processes. Encouraging though this may be, it is necessary to note that the purpose of many of these studies was to examine information retrieval from short-term, or episodic, memory (e.g., Larcker and Lessig, 1983). The type of memories criminologists are interested in are stored in long-term memory. Although long-term memory studies do exist, they have generally been designed to investigate accounts of cognitions during structured problems or neutral tasks, such as solving anagram problems or walking to work (e.g., Ericsson and Simon, 1984). Of course, it is known that events that are themselves pertinent or significant, such as getting married, are generally remembered more clearly than mundane ones, such as walking the dog (Price et al., 1982). Thus, we might expect that the decisions associated with significant incidents, such as getting married or committing an armed robbery, and the factors that prompted them might also be remembered more distinctly. Clearly, this is an area that requires further psychological investigation. In the meantime, many social scientists agree with Agnew (1990), who proposed that "... accounts may be the only way of obtaining accurate information on the individual's internal states and those aspects of their external situation that the individual is attending to" (p.271).

Third, with regard to robbery prevention, the perceptual "inaccuracies" inherent in retrospective interviews are not only useful but might even be imperative. If the purpose of obtaining descriptions of a robber's decision-making operation is to aid in the development of prospective preventive strategies, then it is far more important to understand the rationalizations and justifications that are likely to guide an offender's behavior in the future, rather than those that led to his behavior in the past. Clearly, a robber's current reasoning in relation to committing armed robbery is far more likely to influence his future attitudes toward this crime, and his future behavior, than the attitude he may have held in the past. For this reason, the use of retrospective self-reports to examine the decision making of armed robbers is an essential methodological tool.

Each interview commenced with a discussion of the way in which armed robberies tend to be reported by the media. After this introduction, the first important issue that needed to be resolved was the number of robberies for which the interviewee had been imprisoned. If he had been convicted of more than one robbery, whichever one had taken place earliest in 1990 (the "index offence") formed the basis of discussion.

The interview was designed to elicit descriptions of the offender's decision making throughout the planning and commission of the offence. For instance, each robber was asked to describe the factors associated with the type of crime he had committed and his choice of target. Subjects were asked to discuss why they had become involved in the commission of an armed robbery in 1990, and what modus operandi they had employed and the reasons behind it. They were questioned closely about their attitudes toward violence and their preparedness to use force, as well as the role of risk factors such as the possibility of coming into contact with armed police officers and the likelihood of arrest. Other topics included the source and factors influencing choice of firearm, a retrospective account of the offender's career, including robberies for which they had never been convicted, and, their future intentions, in particular with regard to crime.

RESULTS AND DISCUSSION

Use of Firearms

One of the most important objectives of this study was to establish the degree to which real firearms, capable of discharging live shots that can cause serious injury or death, are actually employed in armed robberies. The official criminal statistics published by the British Home Office suggest that the majority (at least 78%) of armed robberies in England and Wales are conducted with real firearms. The information collected from police files provided a similar picture: 55% of these weapons were seen by witnesses and believed to be real handguns; 12% were seen by witnesses and believed to be real shotguns (all had been "sawn-off"); a further 6%

were known to be real guns (2.4% sawn-off shotguns and 3.6% handguns) as they were recovered afterwards by the police; 11% were known to be imitation guns (ranging from blank-firing replica pistols to rolled-up newspaper in a plastic bag) because they were recovered afterward by the police and found to be incapable of discharging any shot; and 16% were not seen at all by witnesses but the robber's demeanor (such as a protrusion from his pocket or an object in a bag), together with either a demand note (10%) or a verbal demand (6%), gave the victims the impression that he possessed a firearm. Thus, according to police records, 73% of the guns used in robberies in the MPD in 1990 were either known or _believed_ to be real.

It is likely that a proportion of the guns reported to be real were in fact imitations. This could be true particularly in the case of handguns because some replica pistols are so realistic that it is difficult, even for firearms experts, to distinguish them from the genuine article on the basis of appearance alone. Thus, it would not be surprising if lay persons assumed them to be real, especially when one considers that they were seen—probably for a matter of seconds—in the highly charged context of an armed robbery.

Because we could tell so little from police records about what proportion of firearms used in robberies had been genuine and loaded, all of the 88 interviewed robbers were questioned closely about the type of gun they had used in the commission of the crime. In four cases the interviewee neither carried anything resembling a gun nor intimated to victims that he possessed a gun, the weapon being carried by an accomplice. In two of these robberies the accomplice carried a real gun, while the other two involved a replica gun. Of the remaining 84 "gun"-carrying robbers, 17% (N=14) said that they had used a real pistol for the commission of the offence, all of which were loaded with live ammunition; 24% (N=20) said that they had used a real sawn-off shotgun for the commission of the offence, of which 14 were loaded and six unloaded; 37 per cent (N=31) produced a weapon during the offence that bore a close physical resemblance to a real firearm but was, in fact, incapable of discharging live rounds (in all but one of these occasions when a toy shotgun was produced, replica handguns were used); 23% (N=19) produced nothing but intimated from their demeanor, verbal demands, or the contents of a demand note, that they possessed a gun ("simulated" firearms).

Thus, in the light of our findings from interviews with convicted robbers, it appeared that the proportion of real guns used (41%) was just over half of the estimate (73%) based upon our study of police records. Furthermore, 30% of the shotguns had not been loaded. So, the proportion of interviewees who carried guns capable of discharging a lethal shot was just 33%.

Furthermore, of the 44 interviewed robbers who carried "handguns," which must have appeared real to witnesses, just under one-third possessed a genuine and potentially life-threatening firearm. The same was true for two-thirds of shotgun carriers. While the Home Office Research and Statistics Department report that 68% of robberies in the MPD during 1990 involved pistols, our study revealed that only 17% of the robbers we interviewed carried a genuine loaded pistol. It would appear that the official statistics greatly overestimate the number of real firearms used in robbery.

It is also important to note that in all cases where robbers operated a subterfuge, and intimated to witnesses that they possessed a firearm without in fact producing anything resembling a gun, they claimed that they had been in fact unarmed. In all cases where the robber was truly armed the gun was displayed to victims. Of course, it is possible that robbers who did not use real firearms were more likely to be caught and incarcerated, thereby inflating our estimate of the proportionate use of imitation firearms. However, this is unlikely to have been a major factor as the robberies committed by the sample of interviewees appeared to have been representative of serious armed robberies committed in the MPD in 1990.

When asked why they chose the type of firearm they did, it became apparent that those who chose to use real loaded guns did not do so simply because they were easily available. Many robbers believed a real firearm was an essential tool for the kind of target they planned to raid. They believed that in certain circumstances it might be necessary to fire their guns and, therefore, anything other than a genuine loaded weapon would not be adequate. Almost three-quarters of those who used a replica firearm or who adopted a simulated gun claimed that they could have obtained a real gun but decided not to. The usual reasons why a real gun was not taken was because interviewees felt that if they possessed one, then in certain circumstances they might fire it (a risk they were not prepared to take), or they simply felt that a real gun was not necessary for the type of robbery they were planning to commit. Also, almost all of these offenders said that if given a free choice between a replica and a real gun, they would still have opted for the replica.

With regard to crime prevention strategies that may be employed to reduce the incidence of armed robbery, it is difficult to determine what effect this last finding should have. It would be, of course, neither ethical nor humane to suggest that the victims of armed robbers should presume that the firearm with which they are being threatened (even when no gun is visible) is anything other than real and capable of firing a live shot. It is easy to see that if victims believed otherwise they might be tempted to behave in a manner that could put their lives, and the lives of others, in jeopardy. However, this finding is directly relevant to the firearms debate discussed earlier. It suggests that the emphasis upon the availability of firearms, and the effort to curb the rate of armed robbery through attempting to restrict access to these weapons, should be questioned. This is not to say, of course, that legislation against the sale and possession of firearms should be retracted. Firearm scarcity has other advantages. For instance, it has been shown that the type of weapon, even firearms of a lower calibre, has the potential to prevent fatal injuries and accidental shootings in the home (Cook, 1983; Zimring, 1972).

Satisfactory outcomes could be achieved, however, if effort was also spent upon developing other forms of crime prevention techniques. As Grabosky (this volume) points out, "... crime prevention planners should make an effort to understand the systems in which they propose to intervene, and the processes which they propose to disrupt. They should look beyond the superficial, mechanistic doctrines of opportunity and deterrence, and understand the psychological processes, social organization and economic systems in which target behavior is embedded" (p.). The purpose of the remainder of this paper is to examine one such "psychological process" that relatively few researchers have so far cared to exploit. The first decision that all offenders must undertake, regardless of whether they are contemplating robbery for the first time, is a seasoned offender, is whether to commit the crime at all. To examine the factors that influence this decision may prompt numerous preventive opportunities.

The Rewards of Armed Robbery

The financial benefits of carrying out an armed robbery are not purely dependent upon the absolute amount of cash gained, but are relative to the needs and expectations of the individual robber. The rewards of robbery were, therefore, expected to be dependent upon satisfactory rather than optimal outcomes. For example, while the sum of £500 may be sufficient to satisfy the immediate needs of a drug addict, it is unlikely to fulfil the requirements of an aspiring jet setter.

To investigate these issues, the robbers were asked to provide three figures: the minimum price (MP)—the minimum amount of money for which they would have been prepared to commit the index robbery); the expected gain (EG)—the amount they personally expected to obtain from the robbery); and the actual profit (AP).

It was hypothesized that the important factors influencing the offender's evaluation would not be the amounts themselves but the difference between the anticipated sum and reality. Thus, the following hypotheses were developed to test the notion that robbers are rational calculators:

- EG would have to be greater than MP for crime to occur.
- If AP was less than EG, the outcome would be viewed as financially unsatisfactory.
- If AP was greater than EG, the outcome would be viewed as financially satisfactory.

In concordance with our first hypothesis, all offenders who had decided upon an MP for which they would have been prepared to commit the robbery expected the index robbery to equal or exceed this value. Had they expected to gain less money than they were prepared to "work for," then as rational decision makers they would not have committed that particular crime at all. Their minimum amounts were, however, quite modest. Twenty-two per cent stated that they would have considered the offence to have been worth carrying out even if they had thought that it would yield less than £500, 19% set between £500 and 1,000 as their minimum, 28% decided on £1,000 to 5,000, while 32% said they required a personal share of at least £5,000 before they would consider becoming involved in such an offence. Furthermore, it was not surprising to find that they generally chose targets that reflected the gains they hoped to achieve. Those with the greatest financial expectations attacked targets likely to yield the highest amounts (such as cash-in-transit vans), while those with less expensive requirements attacked less lucrative targets (such as banks, building societies or stores). But what was, perhaps, more surprising was the accuracy with which they appeared to have "estimated" the *actual amounts* of money *taken* from the different institutions robbed. Analysis of the police files covering the period throughout which these robbers were active in the London area revealed that their financial expectations of the targets they attacked were broadly in line with the median annual losses sustained by those different categories of targets. Thus, their expectations appeared to have been based upon a realistic appraisal of the odds.

It was also hypothesised that if the amount of money obtained by the offender exceeded the amount he had expected to receive, then the offence would be regarded as financially worthwhile. Indeed, having exceeded his expectations, the offender would have received a "bonus," or an extra sum of money that he had not known he would obtain. On the other hand, if the amount of money obtained by the offender was below his expected amount, then the offence would not likely be viewed as having been worthwhile.

Indeed, three-quarters of the interviewed robbers claimed to have obtained more money from the robberies than the minimum for which they would have been prepared to commit the crime, and 54% said that their expectations had been equalled or exceeded. So, in over half of the cases studied, the profit obtained from the robbery more than satisfied the offender's needs. Not surprisingly, then, almost all of these robbers evaluated the offence as having been financially worthwhile (aside from the fact that they were eventually caught and punished for their crime). On the other hand, two out of three offenders whose expectations had not been realized claimed that, had they known how small a profit they would make, they would not have carried out the crime at all. It is unfortunate, in retrospect, that those who obtained less profit than they had anticipated but still claimed to be satisfied with the outcome were not questioned further about the source of their satisfaction.

Therefore, although *we* might expect the financial yield of a robbery to be unpredictable, most robbers appeared to be able to make fairly precise appraisals of the likely outcome. Furthermore, they appeared to plan their raids in order to increase the probability that the gain would closely reflect their expectations. In addition to choosing particular types of targets, as discussed above, careful timing was also employed to increase the probability of as large a yield as possible. For instance, almost a quarter of all raids on jewelry stores took place in the month of December, which may be related to the stockpiling of jewelry in anticipation of increased Christmas sales. Some robbers claimed to have timed their crimes to correspond with certain periods, e.g., when financial institutions increased the amount of money held at each counter in anticipation of the "weekend rush," or on "pension day," before pensioners arrived at post offices.

The Costs of Armed Robbery

Despite the rational consideration the robbers appeared to dedicate to maximizing the potential rewards of the offence, they appeared to put less effort into examining the possible costs incurred in committing an armed robbery. This disregard, furthermore, was not due to any lack of awareness of the potential costs involved. The majority of those interviewed claimed to have been well aware of the sentence likely to be imposed for this type of crime, and almost all were aware of the presence of armed response vehicles in London and of armed police. Further, over 90% claimed to have believed that had armed police chanced upon them during the robbery, there would have been a very high probability that they would have been shot —an event that is, in fact, still an extremely rare occurrence in Britain. Awareness of the risks inherent in the commission of crime is often presented as evidence of the apparent *irrationality* of those acts. On the contrary, such conclusions may merely be indicative of what Walsh (1986) refers to as "differing conceptions of rationality," whereby criminal acts may be regarded as within the realm of rational behavior provided the realization prevails that by its very nature, crime incurs risks and errors thus are an inevitable feature. Even fully "knowledgeable" decisions may come unstuck as a result of the risky and unpredictable nature of many human activities, not least of all criminal ones. Walsh (1986) further points out that rationality does not invariably "work" in the non-criminal world either, where failure tends to result in an acknowledgment of the role of risk as opposed to a denial of rationality prior to the event.

Despite this knowledge of the potential pitfalls of their crime, most offenders claimed to have given little thought to the sentence they could have been facing when planning the crime. Furthermore, most claimed that even if the term of imprisonment they had been likely to receive was twice current levels, it would have made no difference to either their intentions or their modus operandi. Many robbers also claimed that if all British police were armed, their decision would not have been altered. Is this really the behavior of rational decision makers?

It must be remembered, however, that these men were assessing the probabilities of risks, not certainties. If the probability of arrest, a long sentence or being shot is perceived to be very high, then the costs of committing robbery may well be seen to outweigh the benefits and the crime will not occur. On the other hand, if the probability attached to the risks is perceived to be very low, they may well fail to outweigh the benefits of the crime, making it more likely that the crime would occur. Several studies have shown that while certainty of legal punishment is an effective deterrent, severity of legal punishment is not (e.g., Tunnell, 1992).

Indeed, few of the interviewed robbers believed that there was a high, or even a 50-50, chance of armed police arriving at the scene of the crime in time to either arrest or shoot them. Thus, although the presence of armed police was recognized as a risk, it was regarded to be such an unlikely eventuality that the threat was effectively "neutralised." Also, two-thirds of the robbers felt that the probability of being arrested for the offence had been low, as the speed at which these offences take place made it unlikely that the police would arrive on the scene quickly enough to arrest them. Moreover, believed that after they had left the scene of the crime, their chances of being apprehended diminished sharply. Although 84% of these robbers were, in fact, arrested after they had left the scene of the crime, almost half of the interviewees attested to having committed at least a further five armed robberies for which they had never been convicted. Thus, in spite of their current predicament, this judgment was not, in some cases at least, ill-founded.

Correspondingly, the risk of a long sentence was no deterrent as it was believed to be highly unlikely that things would come to that. Even capital punishment is no deterrent to those who believe "it will never happen to me." The lack of weight given to the risks associated with their crimes weakens the case for deterrent sentences as a strategy for controlling robbery, as steep penalties are unlikely to deter those who do not believe they will be caught (Feeney, 1986). Correspondingly, the interviewed robbers were pessimistic about the deterrent effect of target hardening and tougher penalties. Indeed, Gabor et al. (1987) also found that North American robbers were not as responsive to target security measures as advocates of opportunity-reduction strategies might like to suppose. In addition, several writers—though few as poignantly as Sherman (1993)—have addressed the difficulty of making deterrence work. Of course, even if the interviewed offenders were not deterred, it is not known how many other *would-be* robbers have been dissuaded by such crime prevention strategies. Furthermore, even if opportunity reduction measures have little effect upon the robber's decision to attempt a robbery, they may result in the attempt being unsuccessful and/or the robber later being caught and convicted (Morrison and O'Donnell, 1994). Indeed, situational crime prevention methods, such as geographical layout of premises, surveillance and other prevention hardware, achieve to some degree all of these objectives. Thus, their installation may lead to an important deterrent effect in the longer term.

Once again we compared the robbers' predictions with the picture provided by the police reports and we discovered that, although subjective, the assumptions made by these robbers were not unrealistic. Given that the police very rarely arrive while a robbery is in progress (2% of robberies or attempted armed robberies in London in 1990), and that clear-up rates for robberies are well below 50% (and for some categories of target, particularly those without photographic security, it is much lower), it would appear that the offenders were making well-founded and rational inferences with regard to the costs associated with armed robbery.

It is of interest to note also that many of the practical aspects of the robbers' modus operandi were not employed merely as a way of maximizing the financial takings (although this certainly appears to have been a secondary consideration, as mentioned earlier), but also served as "risk reduction strategies." The timing of the robberies was often chosen to coincide with the quietest time of the day; targets were approached specifically when empty in order to reduce the number of possible witnesses or "have-a-go heroes" who might attempt to intervene. Some robbers even claimed to have chosen a time when rush-hour traffic would be likely to interfere with the speedy arrival of police. Walsh (1986) recognized a process that is undoubtedly related to the risk-reduction strategies employed here. He described the way in which economic criminals attempt to locate the "window of vulnerability"—the flaws in the "impregnable" security that protects the target. Both processes are not only rational attempts to control the likely outcome but will shape the modus operandi and determine the choices made.

Walsh (1986) also recognised, during his analysis of the victim selection procedures of robbers and burglars, that offenders place a great deal of emphasis on the role of intuition and hunches that may or may not be based on past experience. He found that, even when faced with failure, economic criminals will attribute an unprecedented outcome to bad luck and fatalism. Most of the offenders interviewed for the purposes of this study also blamed their arrest and conviction on bad luck or informants rather than on good investigative policing or their own mistakes. The most important point about this, however, is that they would have found no reason to alter their perceptions of police effectiveness (which was, anyway, quite negative) in the light of their arrest and subsequent conviction. What this means is that, if there was a "next time," they would be unlikely to perceive the potential costs of the offence to be any greater. Harding and Blake (1989) referred to a similar demonstration of "fuzzy logic" during their analysis of weapon choice by Western Australian robbers—a phenomenon Harding later described as a "'deterrence hiatus'—a rationality gap between the expectations and the consequences of chosen behaviours and between past experience and future intentions," so that, "despite what one would have thought would be the shattering of their illusions, [the robbers] overwhelmingly asserted that they would continue to use firearms as the crime weapon when committing their next robbery offence" (Harding, 1993:97). It would appear that if an offender's original rationale for committing the crime, or for adopting a particular modus operandi, remains intact (due to external attribution of blame for the unexpected and undesirable outcome on this occasion), there is little reason for him to alter his perceptions or, indeed, his future behavior.

CONCLUSION

The findings of this study do not bode well for preventing armed robbery. Exclusive focus upon the issue of firearms and their availability, at the expense of exploring other preventive strategies, may not be justified as our results suggest that, in Britain at least, a significant proportion of "armed" robberies may not be carried out with real guns. In addition, it appears that robbers rarely base their assessment of weapon choice upon the issue of availability alone. Neither did those who chose not to use a real firearm base this choice upon the potential to receive some degree of court leniency, in the event of their arrest and subsequent conviction. Thus, longer sentences for the use of "real guns" would not be expected to have much impact upon offenders' decisions to commit robbery. Of course, this is much as we would expect, given that these robbers were rarely found to consider the eventuality of capture and regarded it to be of minor importance.

Correspondingly, the decision to carry out the armed robbery seemed to be a robust one. The mental equation to assess the pros and cons of committing the crime of armed robbery was, for these robbers at least, heavily weighed in favour of "the pros." Of course, it is not possible to determine how many potential robbers there were whose calculations led them to quite a different conclusion. One of the major limitations of studies such as this one is that they are based upon interviews with the undeterred and the failures (at least on this occasion). However, to redress the balance in order to achieve a more favourable outcome with regard to these undeterred robbers would clearly be no easy task. It does not seem possible, or practical, to increase the law enforcement effort aimed at this crime. Even though to do so may help alter robbers' perceptions of the certainty of arrest to some degree, it is likely that very large increases in criminal justice input would be required in order to deliver even small gains in overall clear-up figures. It is also true that other factors impinge upon police efficiency. For instance, public assistance is important in order to identify robbers; the motivation of employers to install preventive hardware (and ensure that it is properly maintained) and to train staff in techniques of robbery avoidance is imperative if prevention is to succeed at all.

Neither does it seem practical to expect financial institutions and commercial properties to reduce counter cash much more than they already have. Anyway, as the results of this study show, some of today's robbers are generally satisfied with, and are prepared to commit robbery for, very small amounts of money. Thus, with regard to reducing the financial incentive to rob, there does not appear to be a simple or satisfactory solution.

If armed robbers are not going to be deterred by either reducing the size of the rewards or increasing the prospect of arrest (and other associated risks), then possibly the best avenue to pursue would be that of target hardening and other situational crime prevention strategies. It has been suggested that the effects of such strategies may reach beyond primary deterrence (preventing the robbery from being attempted at all) into the sphere of secondary prevention (foiling the attempt to rob) and subsequent detection of offenders. What is also required, however, is further study of the dynamics of robbers' interpretations in order to pinpoint the essential elements of the motivation to rob.

In this respect, it is important to acknowledge that individuals do not make the decision to rob in a social vacuum but are influenced by predisposing factors outside the immediate context, such as social learning and experience and other driving forces (Cornish and Clarke, 1986; Feeney, 1986; Gabor, 1988; Harding, 1993; Wright and Rossi, 1986). How do people develop the readiness to commit armed robbery? How do offenders obtain their information about this crime? Perhaps from this kind of analysis, we can develop a clearer understanding of armed robbery and the processes that might prevent it. Indeed, despite the recent fashion of adopting crime-specific—as opposed to person-centered—analyses of crimes such as robbery, all of the writers who support this approach acknowledge the inevitable role of personal factors. As Feeney (1986) points out, "Logically the decision to rob is a very complex matter involving the whole past of the individual considering the crime as well as that person's present situation" (p.54-55). Only by examining these factors does it seem possible to derive effective early preventive techniques.

There are many other factors that also influence an offender's decision to commit armed robbery. For instance, we have made no mention of one of the most important factors to have instigated this decision-making analysis—the motivations behind the crimes. All of the offenders claimed to have a motivation, and many believed that their motivations would have encouraged anyone (or anyone in the same circumstances, at least), to have done what they did. Those who had an addiction to feed or had severe financial burdens may have regarded this crime to be the best alternative available to obtain sufficient amounts of money quickly. Even when the amount of money obtained was quite small (an element often touted in support of the irrationality of economic criminals), it must be recognized that even apparently small sums may be adequate for the offender's immediate needs. Hence, gains may be subjectively much larger than they appear (Walsh, 1986). Those who were tempted by a "desirable lifestyle" (one in five offenders) may have had no other way of obtaining the 'symbols of success' that are held in such high esteem in our society. Furthermore, most of the individuals interviewed had embarked on a life of crime sometime before their entrance into the 'big league' of armed robbery.

In this context, the subjective interpretations of these individuals may be viewed as logical calculations based on a history that allows offending to be within the boundaries of their personal sensibilities; an immediate motivation, or need, requiring a timely solution; but also, their interpretations may be viewed to be based on a reasonably well-founded, balanced and accurate appraisal of the odds.

◆

Acknowledgements: We are indebted to many people from a variety of organisations for their cooperation and assistance throughout the study upon which this paper is based. The collection of data from police files was completed by Alison Bone, Jeremy Hopgood, Albert Marshall and Lisa Marshall. The staff at the Metropolitan General Registry, the National Identification Bureau, the Metropolitan Police Forensic Science Laboratory, Scotland Yard and in 32 prisons and young offender institutions throughout England and Wales were all extremely helpful.

We are most grateful to Peter Southgate of the Home Office Research and Planning Unit. At the Centre for Criminological Research, we are especially grateful to Sarah Frost and Sylvia Littlejohns, and to Roger Hood, the Director of the Centre, for his assistance and support.

Most of all, we would like to express our sincere thanks to the armed robbers without whose participation this research would not have been possible.

NOTES

This paper is based on a study commissioned by the U.K. Home Office. The research was carried out at the Oxford University Centre for Criminological Research.

1. A number of researchers have attempted to analyse offenders' decision making within a rational choice perspective. For examples see Bennett and Wright (1984), Cromwell, Olson and Avary (1991) and Maguire and Bennett (1982) on burglars; Caroll and Weaver (1986) on shoplifters; Light, Nee and Ingham (1993) on car thieves; Harding and Blake (1989) on violent offenders.

2. For the findings on these issues, and on weapon choice in particular, see Morison and O'Donnell (1994).

3. According to the Theft Act 1968 (sec. 8.1), "A person is guilty of robbery if he steals, and immediately before or at the time of doing so, and in order to do so, he uses force on any person or puts or seeks to put any person in fear of being there and then submitted to force."

4. Defined by the Firearms Act 1968 (sec. 57.1) as, "... a lethal barrelled weapon of any description from which any shot, bullet or other missile can be discharged ..."

5. Defined by the Firearms Act 1968 (sec. 57.1) as, "... any thing which has the appearance of being a firearm... whether or not it is capable of discharging any shot, bullet or other missile..."

6. These interviews were discarded because: the inmate had been mistakenly identified and was serving a sentence for an offence other than robbery; or the interviewee maintained that he was not guilty of the robbery and had been wrongfully convicted; or the interviewee appeared to be suffering from psychiatric problems and was unable to offer any useful information.

7. The distinguishing characteristics of robbers who employed different types of weapons are described in Morrison and O'Donnell (1994).

8. It is important to note, however, that the Home Office figures are based on all robberies recorded by the police, while the present study focused on the more serious armed robberies that had been dealt with by the Flying Squad. Thus, the Home Office figures and our own are not directly comparable.

9. During the year in question, the average loss during raids on security vehicles was £20,000 (i.e., around A$40,000), whereas building societies lost just over £1,000 on average and Totalizator Agency Boards, bottle shops and other kinds of shops generally lost less that £500.

REFERENCES

Abelson, R.P. and A. Levi (1985). "Decision Making and Decision Theory," In: G. Linzey and E. Aronson (eds.), *The Handbook of Social Psychology, 1*, (3rd ed). New York, NY: Newbury Award Records.

Agnew, R. (1990). "The Origins of Delinquent Events: An Examination of Offender Accounts." *Journal of Research in Crime and Delinquency* 27:267-294.

Akers, R.L. (1990). "Rational Choice, Deterrence and Social Learning Theory in Criminology: The Path Not Taken." *Journal of Criminal Law and Criminology* 81:653-676.

Barr, R. and K. Pease (1990). "Crime Placement, Displacement, and Deflection." In: M. Tonry and N. Morris, *Crime and Justice: A Review of Research*, vol. 12. Chicago, IL: University of Chicago Press.

Bennett, T. and R. Wright (1984). *Burglars on Burglary: Prevention and the Offender.* Aldershot, UK: Gower.

Berger, P.L. and T. Luckmann (1971). *The Social Construction of Reality: A Treatise in the Sociology of Knowledge.* Middlesex, UK: Penguin University Books.

Berry, N. (1991). *A Shot in the Dark: Firearms Legislation.* Unpublished B.A. thesis submitted to the Council for National Academic Awards, Polytechnic of Wales.

Cannell, C.F. and R.L. Kahn (1968). "Interviewing." In: G. Linzey and E. Aronson (eds.), *The Handbook of Social Psychology* (2d, ed.).   , MA: Addison-Wesley.

Carroll, J. and F. Weaver (1986). "Shoplifters' Perceptions of Crime Opportunities: A Process-Tracing Study." In: D. Cornish and R. Clarke (eds.), *The Reasoning Criminal: Rational Choice Perspectives on Offending.* New York, NY: Springer-Verlag.

Clarke, R.V. (1983). "Situational Crime Prevention: Its Theoretical Basis and Practical Scope." In: M. Tonry and N. Morris (eds.), *Crime and Justice: An Annual Review of Research,* vol. 4. Chicago, IL: University of Chicago Press.

—— (1992). *Situational Crime Prevention: Successful Case Studies.* Albany, NY: Harrow and Heston.

Cook, P.J. (1980). "Research in Criminal Deterrence: Laying the Groundwork for the Second Decade." In: N. Morris and M. Tonry (eds.), *Crime and Justice: An Annual Review of Research,* vol. 2. Chicago, IL: University of Chicago Press.

—— (1983). "The Influence of Gun Availability on Violent Crime Patterns." In: M. Tonry and N. Morris (eds.), *Crime and Justice: An Annual Review of Research,* vol. 4. Chicago, IL: University of Chicago Press.

Cornish, D. and R. Clarke (1986). *The Reasoning Criminal: Rational Choice Perspectives on Offending.* New York, NY: Springer-Verlag.

Cromwell, P.F., J.N. Olson and D.W. Avary (1991). *Breaking and Entering: An Ethnographic Analysis of Burglary.* Newbury Park, CA: Sage.

Ericsson, K.A. and H.A. Simon (1984). *Protocol Analysis: Verbal Reports as Data.* Cambridge, MA: Massachusetts Institute of Technology Press.

Feeney, F. (1986). "Robbers as Decision Makers." In: D. Cornish and R. Clarke (eds.), *The Reasoning Criminal: Rational Choice Perspectives on Offending.* New York, NY: Springer-Verlag.

Gabor, T. (1988). "Armed Robbery Overseas: Highlights of a Canadian Study." In: D. Challenger (ed.), *Armed Robbery.* Canberra, AU: Australian Institute of Criminology. (Seminar Proceedings No. 26.)

—— M. Baril, M. Cusson, D. Elie, M. LeBlanc and A. Normandeau (1987). *Armed Robbery: Cops, Robbers and Victims.* Springfield, IL: Charles C. Thomas.

Greenwood, C. (1972). *Firearms Controls: A Study of Armed Crime and Firearms Control in England and Wales.* London, UK: Routledge & Kegan Paul.

Haran, J.F. and J.M. Martin (1984). "The Armed Urban Bank Robber: A Profile." *Federal Probation* 48:47-73.

Harding, R.W. (1993). "Gun Use in Crime, Rational Choice, and Social Learning Theory." In: R. Clarke and M. Felson (eds.), _Advances in Criminological Theory_, vol. 5. New Brunswick, NJ: Transaction Press.

—— and A. Blake (1989). _Weapon Choice by Violent Offenders in Western Australia: A Pilot Study_. Nedlands, WA: University of Western Australia Crime Research Centre. (Research Report No. 1.)

Health and Safety Executive (1993). _Draft Guidance on the Prevention of Violence to Staff in Banks and Building Societies_. London, UK: author.

Hessing, D.J. and H. Elffers (1995). _The Validity of the Self-Report Method in Rule-Violating Research_. Paper for Internet Conference. Mailgate.

Indermaur, D. (1994). _Violent Property Crime_. Nedlands, WA: Australia Crime Research Centre, University of Western Australia. (Research Report No. 11.)

Kapardis, A. (1988). "One Hundred Convicted Armed Robbers in Melbourne: Myths and Reality." In: D. Challenger (ed.), _Armed Robbery_. Australian Institute of Criminology. Canberra, AU: Australian Institute of Criminology. (Seminar Proceedings No. 26.)

Kleck, G. (1991). _Point Blank: Guns and Violence in America_. New York, NY: Aldine de Gruyter.

Larcker, D.F. and V.P. Lessig (1983). "An Examination of the Linear and Retrospective Process Tracing Approaches to Judgment Modelling." _The Accounting Review_ 73 (1):58-77.

Light, R., C. Nee and H. Ingham (1993). _Car Theft: The Offender's Perspective_. Home Office Research Study No. 130. London, UK: Her Majesty's Stationery Office.

Maguire, M. and T. Bennett (1982). _Burglary in a Dwelling_. London, UK: Heinemann.

Maybanks, A.S.H. (1992). _Firearms Control: An Examination of the Effects of Present Legislation and the Provenance of Firearms Used in Armed Robberies in the Metropolitan Police District_. Unpublished M.A. thesis submitted to the Faculty of Social Sciences, University of Exeter.

McClintock, F.H. and E. Gibson (1961). _Robbery in London_. London, UK: MacMillan.

Morris, N and M. Tonry (1980). _Crime and Justice: An Annual Review of Research_, vol. 2. Chicago, IL: University of Chicago Press.

Morrison, S. and I. O'Donnell (1994). _Armed Robbery: A Study in London_. Oxford, UK: Centre for Criminological Research, University of Oxford. (Occasional Paper No. 15.)

Newton, G.D. and F.E. Zimring (1969). _Firearms and Violence in American Life_. Washington, DC: U.S Government Printing Office.

Pease, K. (1994). "Crime Prevention." In: M. Maguire, R. Morgan and R. Reiner (eds.), _The Oxford Handbook of Criminology_. Oxford, UK: Clarendon Press.

Polsby, D.D (1994). "The False Promise of Gun Control." *Atlantic Monthly* March:57-70.

Price, R.H., M. Glickstein, D.L. Horton and R.H. Bailey (1982). *Principles of Psychology.* New York, NY: Holt, Rinehart and Winston.

Priest, T.B. and J.H. McGrath (1970). "Techniques of Neutralization: Young Adult Marijuana Smokers." *Criminology* (August):185-194.

Reppetto, T.A. (1976). "Crime Prevention and the Displacement Phenomenon." *Crime & Delinquency* (22):166-177.

Robin, G.D. (1993). *Violent Crime and Gun Control.* Cincinnati, OH: Anderson.

Scott, M.B. and S.M. Lyman (1968). "Accounts." *American Sociological Review* 33:46-61.

Sherman, L.W. (1993). "Defiance, Deterrence, and Irrelevance: A Theory of the Criminal Sanction." *Journal of Research on Crime and Delinquency* 30(4):445-473.

Simon, H.A. (1955). "A Behavioural Model of Rational Choice." *Quarterly Journal of Economics* 69:99-118.

Sutton, A. (1994). "Crime Prevention: Promise or Threat?" *Australian and New Zealand Journal of Criminology* 27(1):5-20.

Sykes, G.M. and D. Matza (1957). "Techniques of Neutralization." *American Sociological Review* 22:667-669.

Tunnell, K.D. (1992). *Choosing Crime: The Criminal Calculus of Property Offenders.* Chicago, IL: Nelson Hall.

Walsh, D. (1986). *Heavy Business: Commercial Burglary and Robbery.* London, UK: Routledge & Kegan Paul.

Walters, G.D. (1994). *Drugs and Crime in Lifestyle Perspective.* Drugs, Health and Social Policy Series, vol. 1. Newbury Park, CA: Sage.

Weatherhead, A.D. and B.M. Robinson (1970). *Firearms in Crime: A Home Office Statistical Division Report on Indictable Offences Involving Firearms in England and Wales.* London, UK: Her Majesty's Stationery Office.

Wright, J.D. and P.H. Rossi (1986). *Armed and Considered Dangerous: A Study of Felons and their Firearms.* New York, NY: Aldine de Gruyter.

—— P.H. Rossi and K. Daly (1983). *Under the Gun: Weapons, Crime and Violence in America.* New York, NY: Aldine de Gruyter.

Zimring, F.E. (1972). "The Medium is the Message: Firearm Calibre as a Determinant of Death from Assault." *Journal of Legal Studies* (1):97-123.

—— and G. Hawkins (1973). *Deterrence: The Legal Threat in Crime Control.* Chicago, IL: University of Chicago Press.